Church History 101

A Concise Overview

CHRISTOPHER M. BELLITTO

Liguori
LIGUORI, MISSOURI

Imprimi Potest:
Thomas D. Picton, C.Ss.R.
Provincial, Denver Province
The Redemptorists

Published by Liguori
Liguori, Missouri
www.liguori.org

Library of Congress Cataloging-in-Publication Data

Bellitto, Christopher M.
    Church history 101 : a concise overview / Christopher M. Bellitto.—
1st ed.
    p. cm.
    ISBN 978-0-7648-1603-1
    1. Church history. I. Title. II. Title: Church history one hundred
one. III. Title: Church history one hundred and one.

BR145.3.B45 2008
270—dc22   2008001886

Liguori Publications, a nonprofit corporation, is an apostolate of the Redemptorists. To learn more about the Redemptorists, visit Redemptorists.com.

Printed in the United States of America
11 10 09 08   4 3 2 1
First edition

In loving memory of
Sr. Dorothy Flanagan, C.N.D.
1920–1997,
who made me better at what I do.

Terrific nun
Cajoling educator
Classy lady

CONTENTS

ACKNOWLEDGMENTS

I am grateful to the team at Liguori Publications, starting with Alicia von Stamwitz, who brought me back to Liguori; Daniel T. Michaels, who encouraged this book's first steps and helped shape its structure; and especially Father Mathew Kessler, C.Ss.R., and Judy Ahlers, who made the final steps in the process happen with skillful editing and professional efficiency. My thanks also go to the copyeditors, proofreaders, and designers, particularly Jodi Hendrickson.

Several people offered gentle and careful advice after reading drafts. I thank specifically my brother, Anthony Bellitto, the proverbial target reader; and Father Francis J. Corry, my first church history teacher, from whom I have never stopped learning. Finally, and as always, I thank Karen Bellitto, my wife and my best friend, for being her and for helping me be me.

CHRISTOPHER M. BELLITTO

INTRODUCTION

Why read church history? There are many reasons, and one of the best—a classic defense of studying history, in fact—comes not from a Christian but from a pagan Roman statesman with the heart of an historian and the soul of a philosopher. Cicero (106–43 BC) wrote in his *De oratore:* "To be ignorant of what occurred before you were born is to remain always a child. For what is the worth of human life, unless it is woven into the life of our ancestors by the records of history?"

Applying Cicero's advice, this review of church history has a modest goal. Catholics need an adult understanding of their faith and history for its own sake as well as to be able to link the Church's "today" with her past. This overview seeks to help Catholics get started and situated in church history. It is a primer intended to introduce the skeleton of church history to an audience of general readers, parish study groups, RCIA candidates, catechists, and students.

Often, you might read about the "early church" or the "Renaissance popes" without a clear idea of the who-where-when-what-why-and-how of those periods. This slim volume tries to answer a fundamental question—"What did the church look like in this period?"—and to answer that same question four times, following the traditional categorizing of church history into the major headings of the early, medieval, Reformation, and modern Church. You will find that the chunks of centuries among these four headings are uneven chronologically and occasionally overlap a bit. You may also have seen church history divided into other numbers of headings, such as six or seven eras, by ancient, medieval, and modern historians. But to get started, our four headings will suffice because, although deeper study reveals many subtleties (the "high medieval" period, for instance, or "early modern" history), these four eras helpfully illustrate the Church's story at particular points in her life.

Each chapter has a consistent structure or order of elements. Each chapter also includes a straightforward map and timeline to orient the reader in place and period. The timeline will sometimes identify famous events or people not covered in the text to indicate what else was going on in the world—subject matter you might want to pursue after reading this introductory book. Then each chapter addresses the same quartet of topics:

- First, "The Big Picture" steps back to view the period broadly so we will not fail to understand the most important "macro" issues and events at work.

- Second, we examine what "The Church's Hierarchy" (pope, cardinals, bishops, and so on) was doing during this time period.

❧ Third, we look at "The Church in the Pews" to ask what Christianity was like for the average person—not unlike the average reader. These two parts taken together avoid an either/or approach; church history entails neither just the "great men (or women)" approach nor the opinion that the only thing that mattered was what occurred in parishes. By looking at the Church's head *and* her members, to use a theological formula, we will try to see the whole picture and realize that a "both/and" perspective is better than "either/or."

❧ Fourth, having considered many of the same things in each period, we finish by taking a more comparative approach to ask, "What Makes This Period Unique?"

Each chapter concludes with discussion questions and a few accessible works in English for further reading. I have not included footnotes because this is a brief work of synthesis, but my unacknowledged sources include at least those listed.

So now, to follow Cicero's advice, let us enter the records of history.

CHAPTER 1

The Early Church
(ca. 30–500)

Timeline

ca. 30	Jesus' Passion
ca. 49	"Council of Jerusalem" decides how to spread faith to Jews and Gentiles
ca. 64	Peter and Paul martyred in Rome during the persecution of Christians that resulted from Roman Emperor Nero's burning down of the city
70	Jerusalem destroyed by Romans; Jewish diaspora begins
ca. 70–100	New Testament written
79	Mt. Vesuvius buries Pompeii
ca. 100–300	Apologists explain and defend Christianity to pagans
ca. 193–305	Episodic, systematic persecution of Christians, during which time, as it is said, "The blood of the martyrs watered the seeds of the church"
201	Roman Empire makes conversion to Judaism and Christianity a capital crime
250	Roman Emperor Decius declares that every Roman citizen must sacrifice to Roman gods on pain of death
ca. 251–356	Antony of Egypt, influential ascetic, father of Christian monasticism
ca. 260–339	Eusebius of Caesarea, "father of church history"
303–305	Last widespread persecution of Christians, begun under Emperor Diocletian
313	Constantine's Edict of Milan tolerates and favors Christianity
325	First Council of Nicaea
380–381	Christianity made official and only religion in the Roman Empire
381	First Council of Constantinople
ca. 382	Books of the Old and New Testament settled into a "canon." Jerome begins translating them from Hebrew and Greek into Latin (the Vulgate Bible) in Bethlehem
354–430	Augustine of Hippo, bishop and theologian
410	City of Rome sacked
431	Council of Ephesus
ca. 435	Patrick brings Christianity to Ireland
451	Council of Chalcedon
476	Traditional year for end of Roman Empire; bishop of Rome steps into power vacuum

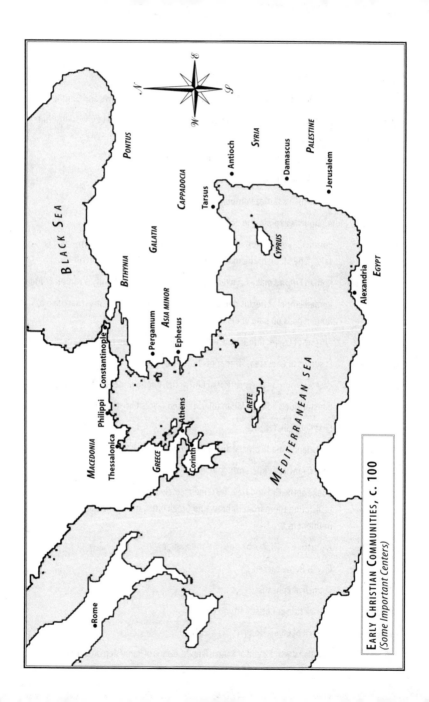

EARLY CHRISTIAN COMMUNITIES, C. 100
(Some Important Centers)

THE BIG PICTURE

Although rooted in Judaism, Greek philosophy, and the Roman Empire, Christianity essentially had to start from scratch. Christians offered the world innovative theological concepts but had few structures to spread the word. Many early Christians were Jews like the apostles and Paul, so they began to preach in synagogues, while gentiles who were not Jews could not at first turn to established churches, bishops, or catechetical programs to learn about the faith. Before any of these situations could develop, Christianity had to establish its identity.

Looking closely at the earliest Roman sources, it appears that they thought the Christians were Jews, which in fact many were in the first years after Jesus. Indeed, we can talk about a "Jesus community" within Judaism in the period following Pentecost, around AD 30. Quickly, however, non-Jewish people became Christians and by the end of the first century we can clearly see a distinct Christianity alongside Judaism and Roman paganism. We hear of *Christianoi*—"men of Christ"—in Antioch as early as AD 40. By 112, a bishop named Ignatius could refer for the first time in history to the "catholicity" of Christianity. He meant the new faith had spread via missionaries throughout the "universal world" of the Mediterranean basin controlled by Rome. Each local church was somehow connected to a larger "worldwide" religion.

The four gospels represent this expanding audience and date to the first century of church history, which is sometimes called the *apostolic period* as distinguished from what followed: the *subapostolic period* ("after" the first apostles). Mark was the first Gospel written, probably in the late 60s or maybe very early 70s, for an audience perhaps once grounded in Judaism but moving rapidly away to include more non-Jews. Matthew's Gospel was written in AD 80–90, more for Jewish Christians and for gentiles who needed to have some Jewish customs explained. At roughly the same time, the author of Luke and The Acts of the Apostles—as a gentile writing for gentiles—emphasized Jesus' role as a *universal* savior. John's Gospel from late in the first century addressed a later generation with different concerns, especially those Christians who were being persecuted as outsiders. Parts of the rest of the New Testament, particularly letters attributed to Paul, predate these gospels, while other writings appeared about the same time or just afterward. Lists of just what books made up the Christian Scriptures circulated from the middle of the second century. By the late 300s, there was a general consensus about which books (twenty-seven in total) constituted the New Testament and it was translated from Greek into the Latin Vulgate—the standard version of the Bible for Christians for a millennium—by Jerome around AD 400.

Romans had a place for Jews within their empire: Judaism was called a *religio licta,* something like a permitted religion, which allowed Jews to practice their faith as long as they didn't make trouble and paid their taxes. Christianity, on the other hand, seemed to be a threat. One of the first things Christians had to do, after explaining their unique belief that Jesus was the Son of God, was to convince Roman officials that they were neither criminals nor a threat to the peace and security of the empire. Enter a group of writers we call *apologists,* referring not to a modern statement of being sorry but to a Greek word for a person who explains or defends a particular position.

Apologists (often also called *Church Fathers,* but including others, among them women) followed several strategies to help establish Christian identity because, like the gospel writers, they were addressing a variety of audiences. Some apologists emphasized Christianity's ties with Greco-Roman philosophy and beliefs while others highlighted the uniqueness of Christianity, paying particular attention to its monotheistic (one-God) faith. And apologists were especially active during the first few centuries after Jesus when the Roman Empire was spreading and then falling (up to the sixth century). Some apologists were zealous, rigid, and self-righteous, but others were open-minded, engaging, and amiable. Most were well schooled in Greco-Roman learning and spoke the language of the educated pagan elite as these apologists tried to convince the Romans that Christians were friends and not enemies of Rome.

Apologists had a range of voices: there were pastoral

preachers and catechists, to be sure, but more typically they spoke rather formally as orators and professors. Their first themes were fundamental, and in the first three centuries after Jesus apologists explained how Christianity was different from paganism and Judaism. Though they typically did not write in a step-by-step, logical way, we learn how creeds, organization, liturgy, sacraments, authority, and Scripture developed by studying their writings. Once it became clear, for instance, that Jesus was not returning immediately—which, apparently, is what the first followers believed fervently—the Church had to exist within the Roman Empire with a structure of its own. It also had to speak to those who opposed the faith as well as to those who were interested in joining.

We can offer a few examples of this subapostolic period of apologetics who helped identify Christians and their beliefs. Justin (ca. 100–165) was a pagan, not a Jew, who became a Christian. His explanations, cool in tone, offered accounts of Sunday eucharistic liturgies and the martyrs who deeply influenced him to the point that he died for the faith, too. Tatian, on the other hand, was an ascetical and uncompromising disciple of Justin who passionately engaged Greek philosophy after his friend's death. A contemporary but anonymous "Letter to Diognetus" focused catechetically on the ways Christianity fulfilled and surpassed Judaism (to the point of being insulting), as well as on how the new faith was not dangerous to Rome because it shared some of the society's better social values. Athenagoras of Athens addressed a "supplication" or "plea" for Christians to the Roman imperial leadership in the late 170s. Christianity was significantly allied with Greco-Roman philosophy, he pointed out, while defending the faith against common slurs that Christians committed incest, engaged in orgies, ate human flesh, and undermined the empire.

Meanwhile, some apologists faced down a challenge, known as Gnosticism, within Christianity itself. Gnostics held that Christianity should be a secret, exclusive religion of a select few. To combat this intramural conflict, Irenaeus (ca. 130–200) in his "Against the Heresies" emphasized that Jesus had come for all, and that the true faith had been handed down from the apostles through the bishops who followed—so we can see apologists by this time defending not only the faith, but an emerging Church structure. We should also note that Irenaeus was bishop of Lyons in what is today southeastern France, indicating how far the faith had spread in a relatively short time.

A second major component of early church history's big picture is the fact that Christianity had to fight for its life in the Roman world. A caricature has Rome killing Christians constantly; the truth is that Christians were subjected to long periods of toleration of varying degrees, which were punctuated sporadically by violent persecutions.

The first major persecution, which took the lives of Peter and Paul, occurred in the city of Rome in 64 during the reign of the unstable emperor, Nero. He scapegoated the Christians for an immense two-week fire that he may have had started himself to make room for a huge palace complex. At this point, Christianity was not legal and was considered a dangerous and evil sect to be monitored closely. For the next hundred years or so, Christians were largely left alone; they were rarely hunted down and, if they came to the attention of Roman authorities, they were given multiple chances to repent. The emperor Trajan (98–117) even gave them a measure of legal due process, ensuring that Christians could not be denounced without evidence or by an anonymous source.

By the reign of Marcus Aurelius (161–180), however, Christians existed in formidable numbers and in every part of the vast empire. Christians acted with rising fervor and had attracted not just a few elite followers, but masses of slaves, women, and the equivalent of the blue-collar middle class. In the provinces especially, Roman officials equated loyalty to Rome with religious piety toward the pagan gods. Christians were increasingly charged with atheism because their belief in one God contradicted Greco-Roman polytheism. More systematic persecutions followed from 193 to 305. In 201, converting to Judaism or Christianity was declared a capital offense, but the more the Romans killed the Christians, the more Christianity grew. Two emperors, Decius (249–251) and Valerian (253–260), began empire-wide persecutions on the most organized scale to date. The Roman Empire at this point was flagging intellectually and its overstretched resources allowed barbarian tribes to nip at the frontiers; once again, Christians were scapegoated as enemies of stability and order. All Christians were ordered to worship the Roman gods by offering a pinch of incense before a statue and eating sacrificial meat. Death was the alternative.

The worst, or "great," persecution started in 303 under Diocletian, whose daughter and wife may have been Christian catechumens. The cause is unclear, although the timing coincided with an increase in religiosity connected with the emperor himself and with another wave of barbarian invasions at the borders. Diocletian fired Christians from public service, destroyed churches, confiscated Scriptures, and demoted Christian aristocrats. The next emperor, Galerius, turned the persecution into an all-out war in 304 when he declared that every Christian must sacrifice to the Roman gods or die. But Galerius experienced deathbed scruples in 311, when he issued an edict of toleration that ended the persecution, freed Christians from prison, and declared that the Christian God could be acknowledged. Fuller toleration followed under Constantine's Edict of Milan in 313, which was the first step toward making Christianity the established religion of the empire. Although other religions were permitted, they lacked Christianity's growing preeminence. In 380 and 381, the emperor Theodosius completed the story by making Christianity the only and official religion of the Roman Empire, while designating all others as heresies.

Christianity had turned the tables. To be a Roman was to be a Christian, while atheists were Greco-Roman pagans. By the end of this early church period, the Roman Empire was just about done. Meanwhile, Christianity had not only survived but had replaced paganism as the religious glue of society. While Western civilization dimmed a bit over the next few centuries, Christianity became a guiding light that burned with increasing intensity and illuminated an ever-widening circle.

THE CHURCH'S HIERARCHY

It would be centuries before the Church had a clear chain of command stemming from Rome. Better to think of the early church as a widespread collection of individual Christian communities connected by the faith and corresponding with each other through charismatic leaders who spoke for each community. Various words without precise meaning were used for these leaders: the Latin words *presbyter* and *sacerdos* came to denote priests, while the Greek *episcopos* and the Latin *episcopus* began as common words for supervisor or inspector and were eventually applied to bishops. In the earliest years, these words appear to have been used interchangeably for the men operating in what would later be clearly bishops' or priests' jobs.

Bishops, priests, and deacons likely developed from Jewish elders and the synagogue structure; in fact, sometimes the people identified—perhaps anachronistically—as bishops, priests, and deacons were gathered collectively as Christian elders. Early on, the elders were lay leaders who probably served as lectors and catechists, but by the third century this category seems to have been subsumed into the role of deacon. By the third century, when growing numbers of Christians necessitated more than the typical one Eucharist (from the Greek word for giving thanks) celebrated each Sunday by the bishop in large cities, we find priests not only bringing the consecrated Eucharist from the bishop's liturgy but celebrating Mass on their own far from town centers.

Early in the Church's life, each community coalesced around one bishop to create what came to be called *monepiscopacy*. Bishops chose, examined, and ordained priests and deacons; assigned them to what became parishes; took their advice on doctrinal and disciplinary matters; and sanctioned them as teachers and preachers, especially for converts. Assisted particularly by their deacons, bishops functioned as teachers, preachers, judges, and liturgical leaders who also settled theological questions, dispensed charity, and disciplined the community—especially the clergy.

The earliest of these men followed Jesus' apostles, who spread out to preach the gospel, and they in turn were succeeded by others to form the first links in a chain the Church calls *apostolic succession*. How they were chosen is not always clear; it is likely that an apostle or his successor designated who was to follow. There are accounts of communities choosing from among their own as well as a single leader emerging because everyone simply realized he was the right man for the job at a particular place and time. Certain cities, because of their geographic location and social-economic-political status, became more important than others, and this gave greater prominence to the bishops of those cities. Gradually a metropolitan bishop was placed in charge of a city and its suburbs, with other bishops placed above and below that bishop to organically form a hierarchy. The five biggest places came to be led by bishops called patriarchs: Rome, Jerusalem, Alexandria, Antioch, and Constantinople.

A question quickly arose: What was the precise relationship among all bishops as well as among these five patriarchs? More specifically, was there one bishop—perhaps in Rome—who had special standing? If the answer was yes, did this bishop of Rome have more than just higher prestige? Did he, in fact, have some sort of real authority over other bishops? It wasn't long before people realized Rome had a certain special quality, given that it was the city holding the bodies of the martyred Peter and Paul. Away from Rome, most bishops seemed to defer to Rome's uniqueness without abdicating their own jurisdiction. Especially in North Africa, we find bishops asserting that Peter and Rome may be first in line (primacy), but not necessarily first in authority (supremacy). Some local church councils throughout the Mediterranean sent unresolved questions or disputed decisions to Rome for final adjudication, while others may have sent their decisions to Rome simply because that city was a logical hub from which to disseminate news and theological developments.

By the middle of the third century, we find bishops of Rome—over time called *popes*—who were asserting not only their primacy but also their supremacy. The decentralized string of Mediterranean churches was becoming more centralized, at least as far as the bishop of Rome was concerned. Callistus I (217–222) was probably the first bishop of Rome clearly to name Peter as the source of his own authority and Rome's preeminent apostolic succession. Stephen I (254–257) used the powerful phrase *cathedra Petri* (chair of Peter) to refer to his authority. Julius I (337–352) rebuked bishops in Antioch for not informing him first of their decisions. Damasus I (366–384) called other bishops "son" and not the more typical "brother." After the Emperor Constantine protected the Church in the early fourth century and then provided land, buildings, and wealth, the bishop of Rome became both a religious and civil leader, especially after the emperor's power later collapsed and the Roman bishop was left standing pretty much alone in the former imperial capital by the end of the fifth century. The "imperial church," as it is sometimes called, that followed was both a blessing and curse. It was natural, even efficient, to adopt the Roman Empire's administrative structures to the growing church, but the trappings of power that accompanied the Roman influence also had their downside as history would demonstrate.

Meanwhile, some bishops outside Rome believed that all bishops shared in apostolic succession equally, and that Peter's authority may flow through Rome symbolically, but legally the authority of every bishop was the same. For them, "first among equals" referred only to a kind of ceremonial acknowledgment, not to any legal superiority. We find this reading of the tradition especially in the Greek East, where bishops believed the highest decision-making arena was not the bishop of Rome's seat of authority but a general council. Rome may have had greater prestige because of Peter, but this did not translate into greater power; local autonomy, in this scenario, was not to be abandoned.

The issue of papal primacy and supremacy came to a head in 451 at the general Council of Chalcedon, whose agenda about a number of theological matters was set by a letter Pope Leo I (440–461) had addressed to the bishops meeting there. During their deliberations, in fact, the bishops shouted, "Peter has spoken through Leo!" One of the council's statements, or canons, placed the bishop (or patriarch) of Constantinople on equal footing with the bishop of Rome, although acknowledging that Constantinople stood second in line behind Rome. When word of this canon got back to Rome, Leo essentially crossed it out, asserting his authority to do so—a canon was not a canon until the pope ratified it. The bishops of the East, however, had considered the matter settled because they had decided together in council. Leo's subsequent cancellation of this canon was invalid, in their eyes, and a breach of their collective authority or collegiality.

The break between the Latin West and the Greek East, already in the works, fractured all the more after the Council of Chalcedon. Eastern bishops accepted Rome's primacy within the five patriarchates, but rejected the idea that Rome's primacy meant legal supremacy. The Church's government was to be shared by all bishops, but particularly invested in a kind of communal executive administration by the five patriarchs. Eastern bishops rejected the ideas that Rome had universal jurisdiction, that one bishop could overrule another, and that Rome sat over other churches like a mother to a daughter. There were other issues of disagreement: among them, the more familiar included the facts that the West used unleavened bread for the Eucharist while the East used leavened and that priestly celibacy was enforced in the West but not in the East. (To push the story ahead, tensions continued until the Great Schism of 1054 when East and West excommunicated each other. This action was mutually lifted in 1965.)

THE CHURCH IN THE PEWS

The first thing we should say is that there weren't any pews in the early church. Christians met where they could, starting with synagogues if they were Jewish and moving to the equivalent of people's living rooms in what we would call "house churches," not unlike what you might improvise on the dining room table if you asked a priest to say Mass in your home today. Early on, the word *synagogue,* which means gathering, and church or assembly (in Greek, *ekklesia*) were interchangeable. During persecutions, Christians may have met elsewhere, in secret locations that could have included the catacombs, but these were poor places to hide because the Roman authorities knew where they were, and so they were instead used mostly for burials. And there were plenty of burials during the sporadic persecutions: the Church's first heroes were the martyrs. While it is impossible to place a precise number or even a reasonable guess on how many Christians died for the faith, surely there were at the very least tens of thousands of martyred men, women, and children.

After the Roman emperors tolerated and then favored Christianity, martyrdom gave way to asceticism as the model way of life and the best way to achieve the personal conversion (in Greek, *metanoia*) that was at the heart of becoming a Christian in a pagan world. There were both desert fathers and mothers, although, given the social climate of the day, it was easier for men to live alone as hermits. Both men and women also lived in small groups as *coenobites*—that is, alone but in close proximity to each other, or together in small numbers in a shared place. These ascetics (also called *anchorites*) flourished especially in Egypt and Palestine starting in the third century, and clustered in desert huts around natural leaders such as Antony of Egypt (ca. 251–356), who served as a spiritual director for a scattered community. They also lived in caves in the rough hills of Greece, Turkey, Italy, and Sicily. Visitors carried the Eastern tradition of ascetical practices and meditative prayer to the West via biographies, guidelines for living that kind of life (notably John Cassian's early fifth-century *Conferences* and *Institutes*), and handbooks such as *The Sayings of the Desert Fathers,* a collection of proverbs and stories.

About 530, Benedict of Nursia synthesized several hundred years of asceticism into his influential *Rule,* which guided the religious life of laymen and laywomen (still not quite "monks" and "nuns" yet) during the coming Middle Ages and beyond. It was this Rule that led to the familiar aspects of medieval monasticism: the eight times for prayer (called the *opus Dei* or the "work of God"—not the modern religious movement), sacred reading and meditation *(lectio divina),* and the important role of manual labor as a spiritual exercise as well as a way of allowing monasteries and convents to sustain themselves economically.

One could, of course, be a good Christian without dying for the faith or living in a cave or desert hut, but those who did so were held up above the rest. Christians who were not inclined to make such extreme choices adopted less-demanding forms of these choices by periodically fasting, abstaining from sex, or denying something they enjoyed for an extended period of time—a longer form of Lenten practices today. But most of the earliest Christians tried to strike the balance of living in the world without being tempted by its darker side. They spent their time learning about the faith's essentials, teaching others, and practicing a moral life that emphasized virtue and guarded against vice.

Christian life among the laity centered on helping others, learning about Jesus through Scripture, and celebrating the sacraments. (Although these were developing, it wouldn't be until the Middle Ages that the Church officially set seven sacraments for herself.) At first, what we call baptism, first Communion, and confirmation (the sacraments of initiation) were bound together, typically at the Easter Vigil, with some combination of anointing, immersion in water, and receiving the Eucharist. Adult baptism seems to have been the norm for several hundred years, but by the fourth century infant baptism with godparents was on the rise. Adult baptism followed a period of as long as three years of learning the Church's fundamental beliefs (called the *kerygma*), and teaching was as much a spiritual activity as learning. What became the sacrament of penance was, in the beginning, a once-in-a-lifetime event for very serious sins; penances could take up to a year or more before full reconciliation with the community was accomplished, usually on Holy Thursday. Marriage wasn't much more than a blessing, if that; and ordinations to the diaconate and priesthood were composed of a simple laying on of hands and, for bishops, an anointing as well. Anointing of the sick is very hard to find in these first few centuries as an action distinct from other anointings and blessings.

Feast days also developed over time. As Christianity moved away from Judaism, Sunday replaced Saturday (Friday sunset to Saturday sunset) as the Sabbath for the logical reason that it was the day of Jesus' resurrection. Sunday was initially seen as a weekly celebration of Easter as the Lord's Day. In 321, the Roman Emperor Constantine made Sunday a day of rest. Easter's emergence as an annual feast evolved from Judaism's Passover, although Christian communities did not always agree on how to date the celebration. Holy Week probably began in Jerusalem in the fourth century after Constantine and his mother, Helena, built a circuit of buildings there marking Jesus' actions. By the end of the fourth century, we find Lent as a forty-day period of preparation for Easter and the final stage of preparation for catechumens. Ash Wednesday came into being as the inaugural day of the Lenten season about the seventh century.

Christmas was, at first, less celebrated than the Easter event, but it became logical to wonder about Jesus' early life and to work backward and reflect on his birth. December 25 was originally a Roman holiday of the winter solstice, marking the shortest day of the year of the invincible sun-god Helios. In 274, the emperor Aurelian made it an official day off, but for a pagan celebration. No one knows when Jesus was born, but it was natural, logical, and safe to turn the sun-god's festival into the Son of God's birthday. By the 330s, Christians had adopted December 25, and in 529, the Emperor Justinian made it not only an official public holiday, but a Christian holy day, too. While there was no proof that Jesus was born at midnight, the tradition of celebrating midnight Mass began in Bethlehem about 380. The date of January 6 for Christmas also appeared because that was the equivalent of December 25 on the Egyptian calendar followed in the Holy Land. Pope Sixtus III (432–440) reconstructed a Bethlehem manger scene in a Roman church he renovated, moving that practice from East to West, but manger scenes had appeared on Roman catacomb frescoes a few decades earlier. Advent had roots in Gaul and Spain in the fourth century and was fixed as the preparation for Christmas in 567.

The laity also regularly practiced the faith at Mass (at first in the common Greek language) and through Scripture study, which were integrally related. Letters to and from communities, such as Paul's, were surely read aloud within a decade of the resurrection; by the third century we have accounts of people standing while gospel passages were proclaimed. The bishop, and later the priest, then gave a moral exhortation, but Scripture was also studied more closely during an *agape* meeting and meal, which originally was held right before the Eucharist. By around 100, the two were separated:

the Eucharist was celebrated Sunday morning and the *agape* on Saturday or Sunday evening. By the end of the fourth century, the *agape* disappeared, probably because Christianity's new status allowed believers to meet openly and in designated worship spaces that replaced the house churches. The reading, homily, prayers, and discussion connected to the *agape* then moved to Saturday morning. Eventually, this Liturgy of the Word (as we now call it) was combined with Sunday morning's Eucharist to form a recognizable Mass, although this combination may have existed in safe places by the early second century.

WHAT MAKES THIS PERIOD UNIQUE?

It's important to remember that, at the very start of Christianity, preachers and apologists didn't have the luxury of a catechism to flip through for authoritative statements of just what this new Christian belief system held as its articles of faith. The Church in any period operates according to an ancient working principle. In Latin, that principle is *lex orandi, lex credendi*—the law of praying is the law of believing. How Christians pray reflects and shapes what Christians believe. So, to get a sense of how early Christians tried to describe or explain what they believed, historians and theologians must turn to how they prayed, especially by looking at creeds and other theological statements that came out of the first of the Church's general councils. Along with Scripture, these authoritative teachings of the councils combined with papal pronouncements and theological statements were the building blocks of what we call the Church's tradition.

Indeed, what clearly distinguishes this early church period from later ones is that much effort was spent simply trying to describe Christian beliefs taught first by the apostles, then their initial successors, and extending into the apologists. Their words were the first theologies and became the basis for later doctrinal statements. The first problem, of course, is that words can never adequately explain mysteries, such as how God can be one and three persons at the same time or how a virgin became pregnant without having sex. Nevertheless, written creeds became necessary. The second problem is that even when we use words precisely and correctly, all languages have nuances, and *two* main languages were being used by churches to talk about Jesus: Greek in the East and Latin in the West. Sometimes, the two sides were literally speaking a different language as they were trying to explain the unexplainable.

What's fascinating about this period is how statements of doctrine developed: questions led to answers, which were sometimes incomplete and led in turn to new questions, more answers, and further clarifications. A graduate student in theology once captured well this initial struggle to make sense of the faith when she said, at the end of an early church history course, "When I started this course, I thought heretics were the bad guys. Now I realize they had no idea they were heretics at all."

Let's start with the first question that had to be answered as believers spread their faith, "Who is Jesus?" On the one hand, he did human things: he lived and he died, he cried when his friend Lazarus died, he ate and even cooked, he slept, he had long conversations with his friends and wrangled with his enemies, he got angry and trashed the Temple, and the night before he died he was scared of what was to happen and disappointed when his disciples couldn't stay up with him. But Jesus is also divine and performed miracles: he raised the dead; he healed blind, deaf, mute, lame, and sick people; he forgave sins; he controlled the weather; and he came back to life. When he was transfigured, God declared: "This is my Son, my Chosen; listen to him!" (Luke 9:35). So how is Jesus' divinity related to the Father's divinity? (And what about the Holy Spirit?)

Faced with these two aspects of Jesus, some people emphasized the human or divine aspect while some tried to strike a balance. Is Jesus human or divine at all—and how? Is he split fifty-fifty? Is he 100 percent divine when performing miracles but 100 percent human when he died? Is he fully human and fully divine? Is he two people or just one person? A priest from the theological center of Alexandria named Arius (256–336) believed that Jesus was somehow less than the Father because he held that Jesus had been created, while the Father alone was uncreated. Arius described Jesus this way: "There was a time when he was not." In Arius' argument, Jesus is less than the Father and does not know as much as the Father; if he is a son, he is a son by adoption and does not share the divine nature. To keep the theology moving forward, then, this meant that humans had not been saved, because only God can save; and, if Jesus is not God, then his death on the cross did not accomplish the purpose of salvation. Also, for Arius, the Holy Spirit was even less God than Jesus.

As frequently occurs in church history, bishops met in regions to discuss the various ways of describing Jesus, and these small meetings led to larger general councils, culminating in this case with the first general council, held at Nicaea (located in today's Turkey) in 325. There, a group led by Athanasius, like Arius also from Alexandria, attacked the Arian position to emphasize that Jesus is not just a kind of superman, but truly divine. Asked how the Son is equal to the Father, Athanasius answered, "Like the sight of two eyes." Nicaea published a creed, the first church-wide declaration of Christian faith (local statements had existed previously, typically in manuals for catechumens) that asserted several critical concepts, primarily that Jesus is begotten of the Father's very being, not a creature made out of nothing at some time after the Father. This meant that there never was a time when Jesus did not exist: the Father did not predate the Son. We should note that the breakthrough came in using the Greek term *homo-ousios* (one in being/of the same being/of the same substance) even though that word is not found in the gospels, which reminds us that doctrinal statements must often use new terms to try to describe ancient mysteries. Indeed, the very word *theology* comes from two Greek words: *theos* (God) and *logos* (word), so theology is "talking about God."

Nicaea did not settle everything, however, and now the question became: how did the individual persons of Father, Son, and Spirit relate to each other within the unity of the Trinity? This word *trinitas,* possibly used in Latin for the first time by the apologist Tertullian in the second or third century, offers another example of having to invent words that approximate a mysterious truth. Another way of asking this question is to pursue how the Trinity's unity relates to the individuality of its three persons. How do "one-ness" and "three-ness" operate at the same time without being contradictory? Questions especially arose about the Holy Spirit, whom Nicaea left hanging by asserting belief in the Spirit without defining it as the council had done for the Father-Son relationship. Is God only one person at a time—sometimes Father, sometimes Son, and sometimes Spirit—a theological position colorfully termed "modal monarchianism"? Some theologians tried to find middle ground or, in fighting one side of the balancing act, tipped the balance in the other direction. Jesus is "like" but not "the same as" the Father, ran one school of thought, while a theologian named Apollinaris tried so hard to beat back the persistent Arian claim that Jesus is not God that he ended up making it sound as if Jesus is fully divine but not fully human.

Once again, a general council met, this time at Constantinople (today's Istanbul) in 381. This council added to Nicaea's Creed to clarify and explain in greater depth these essential theological truths. The creed recited in every church every Sunday today is not the Nicene Creed, as it is sometimes called as a type of shorthand, but really the Nicene-Constantinopolitan Creed. It states that Father, Son, and Spirit are all co-eternal and co-equal: three separate persons as well as a unified God all the time and all at the same time.

So, by the end of the fourth century, the questions of

Jesus' divinity were pretty much settled, but not necessarily the questions of how that divinity related to his humanity. If Jesus is fully human and fully divine, what did this mean for Mary? Is she the mother of the human Jesus only (*Christokos* in Greek) or truly the mother of God (*Theotokos*)? A monk named Nestorius (ca. 381–451) ended up teaching that Mary is the mother of only the human Jesus because he was trying to steer a course between Arius and Apollinaris. Nestorius' followers carried his thoughts forward when they claimed Jesus must have been human and divine in some separate way—"other and other" was how they put it—making Jesus two separate persons at once: human (son of Mary) and divine (son of God). In time, a third general council, this one at Ephesus (located in today's Turkey) in 431, condemned Nestorianism, although it took a few years for the language to catch up and to be accepted. Jesus was declared to have two natures (one human and one divine) that are uniquely united into one person in a "hypostatic union." Mary is rightly called the mother of God (*Theotokos*).

Still more questions cropped up, following a pattern that can be summed up in modern language this way: "Well, then, if that's true, then what about...?" Another monk, this one named Eutyches, again went too far in the other direction to fight Nestorianism and declared that Jesus is not only one person, but he has only one nature, as well, a position called monophysitism that said Jesus' divinity effectively ate up his humanity. Yet another council, at Chalcedon (also in Turkey) in 451, met to define matters, declaring that Jesus is eternal, the Son of God, the second person of the Trinity, and fully human and fully divine without one nature canceling the other out at any time.

To pause for a moment, let's note the continual construction of tradition that was necessary because theological statements settled some matters but did not fully define other aspects of the faith. This process reminds us that tradition is organic: it grows and develops over time, using new language in an attempt to more accurately reflect eternal truths. There is, in fact, something of a reluctance to keep speaking about mysteries on the part of the council fathers. At Ephesus and Chalcedon the bishops noted their reliance on Nicaea and Constantinople as normative declarations, but also admitted that they were forced to elucidate the statements of these first two councils because questions didn't stop emerging. Taken together, these first four councils of Nicaea I, Constantinople I, Ephesus, and Chalcedon were considered so powerful that Pope Gregory I (590–604) declared them to be as authoritative as the four gospels.

We might be surprised, then, to find that the first four councils didn't put an end to the speculation and gray areas as the Church moved into the start of the Middle Ages. Monophysitism persisted and a second general council at Constantinople in 553 again condemned it and the several spin-offs that had followed even after the statements of Ephesus and Chalcedon a century earlier. Still one card was left to be played: if Jesus is one person with two natures, does he have one unified will or two separate wills—one divine and one human? The position that he has one, called monothelitism, gained adherents after Constantinople II, so a third council met there in 680–681. Constantinople III condemned monothelitism and declared that Jesus is one person with two natures (human and divine), each of which has a separate will (human and divine), all of which are united via the hypostatic union.

Before leaving this unique period of theological development, we should note two developments. First, theology was bubbling throughout the Church, but especially from below. Accounts say that Christians argued about these things in the markets, so theologians and bishops comprising the Church's head were responding to questions from people in the body of the Church. This trickling-up of questions was matched by a trickling-up of deliberations and answers. Local councils met alone, then in regions, and then finally in general councils in which representatives from the wide Church made binding decisions.

Second, the method of decision-making was not satisfactory to everyone. The best example returns us to a part of church history we mentioned earlier in this chapter: the growing split between the Greek East and Latin West. In this case, the issue was the Latin word *Filioque,* which means "and the Son." It refers to the Holy Spirit to say that the Spirit proceeds from the Father *and* the Son instead of the Father alone. Some churches in the Greek East rejected the use of the word *Filioque* not so much for its theology but because of the way the word was— to their eyes—imposed upon the rest of the Church. The word does not, in fact, appear in the documents of Constantinople I (381), but was later added in Latin translations in the West and taken as an article of faith, starting in seventh-century Spain, where Arianism persisted. The word was alternately accepted and rejected in the West— Pope Leo III (795–816) posted the creed without the word *Filioque* in Rome—but by about 1000 the word *Filioque* was routinely used in Western creeds. Eastern bishops objected that the word was added by the West outside the context of a general council where the five patriarchs of Rome, Alexandria, Jerusalem, Antioch, and Constantinople could exercise their shared leadership and collegiality with their brother bishops.

As we leave this early church period, it is essential to remember that perhaps during no period, other than the Reformation to follow a millennium later, has the Church had to spend so much time and effort explicitly figuring out and stating clearly what it is and isn't about.

DISCUSSION QUESTIONS

1. *Did anything about early church history surprise you? If so, what?*

2. *Did anything about the early church strike you as particularly familiar? If so, what?*

3. *What models and lessons might be drawn from the early church for today?*

4. *Do you think the church today should be decentralized? Why or why not?*

5. *How did the centralizing tendencies of Rome help the church face challenges?*

6. *Do you think the attempts to define Jesus led to greater understanding or did they just confuse believers?*

7. *Who were the heroes—and why? Who were the villains—and why?*

8. *Give a portrait of the early church to someone who knows nothing about it. What three main elements would you emphasize? Why?*

9. *When early Christians thought of the word* church, *what would they have had in mind?*

FURTHER READING

Brown, Raymond E. *An Introduction to the New Testament.*
New York: Doubleday, 1997.

Frend, W. H. C. *The Rise of Christianity.* Philadelphia: Fortress
Press, 1984.

Hazlett, Ian, ed. *Early Christianity: Origins and Evolution to
A. D. 600.* London: SPCK, 1991.

MacMullen, Ramsay. *Voting About God in Early Church
Councils.* New Haven: Yale University Press, 2006.

Meier, John P. *A Marginal Jew. Rethinking the Historical Jesus,*
3 vols. New York: Doubleday, 1991–2001.

Merdinger, J. E. *Rome and the North African Church in the
Time of Augustine.* New Haven: Yale University Press, 1997.

Ramsay, Boniface. *Beginning to Read the Fathers.* New York:
Paulist Press, 1985.

Stevenson, Kenneth. *The First Rites: Worship in the Early
Church.* Collegeville, MO.: Liturgical Press, 1989.

Swan, Laura. *The Forgotten Desert Mothers: Sayings, Lives,
and Stories of Early Christian Women.* New York: Paulist
Press, 2001.

CHAPTER 2

The Medieval Church
(ca. 500–1500)

Timeline

ca. 530	Benedict of Nursia writes his Rule, which organizes monasticism for men and women
553	Second Council of Constantinople
ca. 570–632	Muhammad, who establishes Islam
632–732	Islam spreads throughout Holy Land, North Africa, and Iberian peninsula
680–681	Third Council of Constantinople
732	Charles Martel stops Islamic advance into Europe at Battle of Poitiers-Tours
787	Second Council of Nicaea
800	Pope Leo III crowns Charlemagne emperor
869–870	Fourth Council of Constantinople
1054	Eastern and Western churches formally excommunicate each other
1066	Normans invade England
1099	Crusaders take Jerusalem
1123	First Lateran Council
1139	Second Lateran Council
1170	Thomas Becket martyred in Canterbury
1170–1221	Dominic, founder of Dominicans
1179	Third Lateran Council
1181/2–1226	Francis, founder of Franciscans
ca. 1182–1253	Clare, founder of Poor Clares
1187	Muslims, under Saladin, retake Jerusalem
1215	Fourth Lateran Council
	Magna Carta in England
ca. 1225–1274	Thomas Aquinas, scholastic theologian
1245	First Council of Lyons
1274	Second Council of Lyons
1265–1321	Dante Alighieri, Florentine humanist and author of *Divine Comedy*
1305–1378	Papacy in Avignon

1311–1312	Council of Vienne
ca. 1330–1384	John Wycliffe, English theologian and reformer
1337–1453	Hundred Years War between France and England
ca. 1340–1400	Geoffrey Chaucer, English poet and author of *The Canterbury Tales*
1347	Black Death arrives in Europe
1347–1380	Catherine of Siena, spiritual teacher
1370–1415	John Hus, Bohemian reformer (condemned and burned at Council of Constance)
1378–1417	Great Western Schism: two, then three, popes
1414–1418	Council of Constance
1431	Joan of Arc burned at the stake
1431–1445	Council of Basel-Ferrara-Florence-Rome
1441	African slaves brought to Portugal
1453	Constantinople falls to Turks
1455	Gutenberg prints his first Bible
1488	Bartolomeu Dias rounds Cape of Good Hope at tip of Africa, opening sea route to the Far East
1492	Columbus crosses Atlantic Ocean after Muslim Granada falls to Ferdinand and Isabella, completing reconquest of Iberian Peninsula begun in eighth century
1495–1498	Leonardo da Vinci paints *The Last Supper*

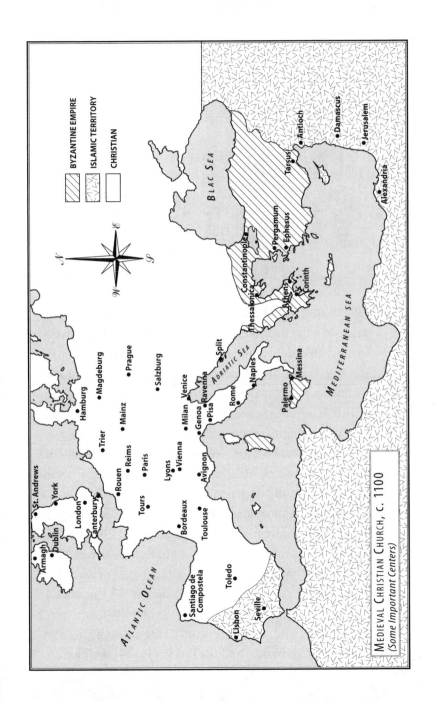

MEDIEVAL CHRISTIAN CHURCH, c. 1100
(Some Important Centers)

BYZANTINE EMPIRE
ISLAMIC TERRITORY
CHRISTIAN

ATLANTIC OCEAN

Armagh
St. Andrews
Dublin
York
London
Canterbury
Rouen
Tours
Bordeaux
Toulouse
Santiago de Compostela
Toledo
Lisbon
Seville

Trier
Hamburg
Magdeburg
Prague
Salzburg
Mainz
Reims
Paris
Lyons
Vienna
Avignon
Milan
Venice
Genoa
Ravenna
Pisa
Split
Rome
Naples
Palermo
Messina

ADRIATIC SEA
MEDITERRANEAN SEA

Thessalonica
Constantinople
Athens
Corinth
Pergamum
Ephesus
Tarsus
Antioch
Damascus
Jerusalem
Alexandria

BLAC SEA

THE BIG PICTURE

We might take a look at these rough dates of 500–1500 for the medieval church and think that Columbus' first voyage in 1492 closed the Middle Ages and began an era of expansion—which, in a sense, it did. But medieval Christianity had already expanded from her early core along the Mediterranean Sea upward throughout all of continental Europe, east as far as Russia, and north as far as the British Isles and Scandinavia. The Roman Empire may have fallen, but Christianity walked in her footsteps.

Christianity became ever more Western, Latin, and Roman because of Muslims. The Church looked northward to expand, driven by the spread of Islam in the seventh and eighth centuries. When the Mediterranean stopped functioning as a Roman lake and became Muhammad's lake, Christianity lost hold of the areas of her first expansion and had to find a second front on which to spread the gospel. Muhammad died in 632 in what is today Saudi Arabia; thereafter, Islam rapidly took control of the Holy Land, Asia Minor up to the gates of Constantinople, North Africa, and the Iberian Peninsula (modern-day Spain and Portugal). In so doing, Islam cut Western, Latin Christianity off from her Eastern, Greek roots, adding a physical breach to what had grown to be a theological and organizational rift between East and West, as we saw at the end of chapter 1. Rome, one of the five patriarchs, was now disconnected from the theological centers of Antioch, Alexandria, and Jerusalem. Constantinople remained unconquered and claimed to be the heir of the Roman Empire until 1453. Yet it had to spend more than seven hundred years worrying about Islam and could offer little help to Roman Christianity. When they did interact, Rome and Constantinople spent more time bickering than cooperating against the common challenge of Islam.

With no hope of help from the places where Christianity first flourished, Rome was forced to look elsewhere for protection. That "elsewhere" was Western Europe because Islam had finally faltered there precisely one hundred years after Muhammad's death. Nearly unrestricted as they marched across the eastern and southern portions of the former Roman Empire, Muslims had crossed the Pyrenees into modern-day France (Roman Gaul), but Charlemagne's grandfather stopped them in 732 at a battlefield between Poitiers and Tours. Because of his effort, this Charles is remembered by history as *Charles Martel*—the Hammer. When his son, Pepin III (also "the Short") needed legitimacy for his claim to power, Pepin asked the pope to intervene. Pope Zachary decided that Pepin should be the king of the Frankish people, and his claim was ritualized by a pair of important symbols: his warriors raised him above their heads on his shield—an ancient secular mark of leadership—and a bishop anointed him. Zachary was happy to be asked to intervene because he saw the request as recognition of his authority in civil as well as religious matters. Pepin was happy to be anointed because it gave his rule a religious overtone.

But here is where the difficulty lies: if the civil ruler had a religious mantle (a kind of sacred kingship) at the same time that the pope was recognized as playing a key role in civil matters, then precisely who was the higher leader in Christian Europe? Who was in charge? The answers were different for kings or emperors, on the one hand, and popes and bishops, on the other. The power struggle between the two was a major part of the medieval Church's big picture, but it was not new. Bishops had been telling Roman emperors and other civil rulers for centuries that they were in the Church, not above it, even as those same civil officials provided the protection, peace, and prosperity that allowed Christianity to expand.

When the next pope, Stephen II, found Rome physically threatened by a people called the Lombards, he turned to Pepin because he knew the Frankish king owed his throne to Pope Zachary. Pepin agreed to drive the Lombards out in return for the pope anointing not only Pepin, but also his sons, and granting him the title "Father of the Romans." The pope also received the territory in central Italy that made up what we call the Papal States; this gift was called the Donation of Pepin and probably extended land that Constantine had given the bishops of Rome more than four hundred years earlier. It was only natural, then, that when Pepin's son—another Charles—came to the throne, he also partnered with the bishop of Rome, Pope Leo III, who crowned Charlemagne ("Charles the Great" after the Latin *Carolus Magnus*) on Christmas Day 800 in Rome. Even more so than his grandfather and father, Charlemagne explicitly took upon himself the mantle of Constantine as defender of the faith and as something of a sacred king anointed by the pope himself. He struck coins and used titles recalling the Christian Roman emperors; he also referred to himself as the vicar of Christ and a thirteenth apostle. Charlemagne identified his empire as the third Rome (after Rome and Constantinople) that was renewing the fallen empire—which led later rulers in the region to style themselves Holy Roman Emperors.

All of this protection was a mixed blessing for the Church. The pope needed physical protection, but not at the expense of the universal recognition of his final authority in religious and civil matters. The Church taught that even the Holy Roman Emperor was a Christian who would be judged in heaven, and the pope believed that he would be called to account for his shepherding of every soul, including the emperor's. Sometimes that necessary protection included fighting attempts by emperors, kings, and local lords to interfere with Church matters, especially naming priests, bishops, and even popes.

This issue is what the famous investiture controversy was all about. Bishops and abbots were invested with symbols of their authority, typically a sword or orb to symbolize their worldly power (since bishops and abbots also controlled land and property) and a miter (hat), crosier (staff), and ring to symbolize their religious authority.

Whoever invested the bishop or abbot appeared to be that person's superior, but the Church argued that religious authority was the higher no matter who did the investing. To combat this problem, the medieval church launched a fight against lay investiture and called for the freedom of the Church to name her own officials. There were as many successes as there were compromises and failures in this fight, but over time the Church did emerge as relatively more independent than before she took up the battle.

It can't be denied, however, that civil leadership starting with Charlemagne allowed the Church to spread the faith, which brings us to another important aspect of the medieval Church's big picture: the evangelization of Europe and the expansion of church structures. This story is really the second chapter of the history of evangelization and shares some elements with the first chapter, when Christianity roared out of Jerusalem and across the Roman Mediterranean world. At that time, too, the apologists had to explain the faith by stressing what Christianity shared with Greco-Roman paganism or by delineating how Christian monotheism stood apart from pagan polytheism. Paul, for example, took the first course when he pointed to a statue labeled "the unknown God" in Athens and announced that the Greeks were already acknowledging the God he preached, to whom he gave the name Jesus (see Acts 17:22–23).

This identification with a sense of the supernatural already in place was exactly the strategy this second wave of missionaries adopted as they pressed Christianity throughout Europe. The credit goes especially to monks from Germany, Britain, and Ireland willing to leave home forever in what they considered the white martyrdom of exile instead of the red martyrdom of a bloody death. They met the remnants of paganism and turned an existing predisposition to religious belief toward Christian faith and practices in innovative ways to produce a lively culture and spirituality. One thinks of Patrick, of course, a fifth-century Brit captured by Irish pirates who, after he returned home to Britain and was ordained a priest, dedicated himself to the Irish culture he'd come to understand during six years of slavery there. While the legend of Patrick's shamrock sermons appears to be just that, they do illustrate the tactic we are discussing: the Irish were surrounded by shamrocks, making its familiar form of three leaves from one stem a natural model to discuss the Trinity.

So, contrary to the popular belief—and occasional slander—Christianity did not mercilessly mow paganism down and impose an imperial church in Europe, but instead tread very lightly. We find that missionaries, at times working on specific advice from Rome, deliberately did not destroy pagan sites. What they did was convert them. Christians might place a baptistery along a river that locals thought contained magical water, for example, or a chapel at the intersection of two roads that naturally formed a cross. For practical reasons—why destroy a shrine you could otherwise use?—some missionaries reconsecrated pagan temples by taking out their statues, sprinkling holy water, and adding an altar for Mass. While the result might lead to an odd mix of paganism and Christianity with little more than a rudimentary understanding of theology toward the end of the first millennium, the Church was nevertheless making important spiritual and cultural inroads on the new frontiers of Europe.

Finally, a third element in the big picture of the medieval church is the explosion of learning. Yes, the third-century apologist Tertullian had famously dismissed Greek philosophy when he asked rhetorically (and disdainfully), "What indeed has Athens to do with Jerusalem? What connection is there between the academy and the church?" But Augustine of Hippo set the tone for the medieval period following his death in the early fifth century. With his *De Doctrina Christiana* (On Christian Doctrine), Augustine cautioned against dismissing the methodology of Greco-Roman education. Christian theologians, liturgists, preachers, and officials required the very skills that the liberal arts had taught for centuries and that had successfully run the Roman Empire. Study of mathematics and astronomy helped plot feast days on calendars; rhetoric made for effective preaching and teaching, especially for bishops; logic and reason helped with theological debate; grammar led to understanding language and literary genres, and therefore the signs contained in Scriptures' words; and music guided liturgy.

The first few medieval centuries were less about intellectual innovation than conservation. It is a cliché but nevertheless true that monks copying manuscripts in dark *scriptoria* preserved pagan Greco-Roman literature, history, and philosophy as well as the first centuries of Christian theology for later generations. Without those monks, the great leaps in learning after the year 1000 could not have taken place. Chief among these store houses of knowledge were Charlemagne's schools, where his advisers oversaw the copying and dissemination of Bibles, writings of the fathers, liturgies, capitularies or laws governing life, monastic rules and stories, and other essential Church documents such as the decisions of the general councils.

Rural monasteries were slowly complemented, and then somewhat replaced, by *cathedral schools* in cities, the new scene of the action because of a commercial and urban revolution about 1100. Bishops gathered around themselves the best-and-the-brightest, who were educated in these cathedral schools. At the same time, guilds of students and teachers formed the earliest universities, beginning at Bologna, Paris, Oxford, and Cambridge. It is here that the scholastic method was developed. A theologian would ask a question and then methodically walk through the reasons why a certain answer was correct and others were incorrect, raising and then addressing contradictions and prior legal and theological statements along the way.

Some examples might help illustrate this development. The most popular training manual was Peter Abelard's twelfth-century *Sic et Non (Yes and No)*, whose very title embodies the scholastic method. The same is true of the most influential collection of canon law, Gratian's *Decretum,* which was published during this period and formally called *A Concordance of Discordant Canons.* The justly famous *Summa Theologiae* of Thomas Aquinas (ca. 1225–1274) was not unique—there were many such summaries of particular sacraments or theological questions—but his was the most comprehensive. Thomas, however, was himself building on the work of his mentor, Albert the Great *(Albertus Magnus,* ca. 1200–1284), who courageously engaged the ideas of pagans such as the ancient Greeks, and of "heretics" such as the Muslims who transported Aristotle from the ancient to the medieval world through Hebrew, Arabic, and Greek texts that were rediscovered in Italy and Spain.

The scholastic method over time devolved into minutiae that were justly labeled as cold and detached *scholasticism.* Although later scholastics never actually asked, "How many angels can dance on the head of pin?" they could have. But it's important to remember that the roots of the scholastic method were practical and pastoral, making *scholastic humanism* a better term to describe the effort to organize questions and answers about the sacraments, especially as they touched everyone's lives through baptism, Eucharist, and marriage. This method, these schools, and their pragmatic concerns produced the popes, bishops, theologians, canon lawyers, and bureaucrats who staffed a revolution in the church's hierarchy.

THE CHURCH'S HIERARCHY

When most people think of the pageantry of the papacy, they have the Middle Ages and the Renaissance in mind, and for good reason. Medieval popes deliberately established the papacy as an institution along the lines of other

especially as the *vicar of Christ,* which reclaimed the latter term from Charlemagne and his successors. They began and ended their letters by referring to their apostolic authority. Statues and mosaics of Peter, specifically of him receiving the keys of his authority from Jesus, found their way into many churches as local reminders of Christianity's headquarters in Rome, where Peter's successors still sat. Second, they deliberately challenged imperial and other civil leadership by deposing bishops and abbots who owed their jobs to a secular ruler instead of a papal or other Church appointment. Popes even deposed emperors and released their followers from feudal oaths of obedience to them to stress the papacy's ultimate responsibility for all matters, both religious and worldly. Third, they created a bureaucracy in Rome that was more organized, deliberate, and structured than the more haphazard machinery that had evolved without much planning and intent during the Church's first millennium, particularly in the five hundred years after the Roman Empire fell.

Fourth, and perhaps most important, popes shaped the College of Cardinals, which already existed in a loose way, into a body of the highest advisers not unlike a royal court. At any one time in the Middle Ages, there were just a few dozen cardinals, but they headed Rome's key offices and acted as papal ambassadors for the most delicate diplomatic and theological tasks as part of this papal revolution. Perhaps most important for this story, the cardinals received the sole right to elect popes. For centuries Roman families and the local clergy had essentially controlled the selection of the bishop of Rome. But if the pope wanted the investiture controversies to go away, he had to make sure that his own election was the best example of an independent choice. The road to the conclave and to the cardinals' exclusive right to elect the pope began with Pope Nicholas II, who, in 1059, assigned the cardinals the leading role in electing, though it remained true that the local clergy in Rome had a hand in it, and that the sitting pope could indicate his choice for a successor. About a hundred years later, a general council called Lateran III (1179) reserved the election to the cardinals alone and stipulated that a two-thirds majority, not the prior unanimous vote, would be sufficient for a valid election. Then, about another century later, the general council known as Lyons II in 1274 gave the Church its conclave, in part because the pope at the time had been elected after nearly three years, and only then after laypeople had locked the cardinals in a room and forced them to choose. Since it worked in his case, Gregory X (1271–1276) applied the process to future elections, now called conclaves since the cardinals were locked up with a key (in Latin: *cum clave*).

The results of all of these developments had pros and cons. The papal revolution produced a papal monarchy that was, in some ways, a sensible development. Once the Roman Empire fell, the Church stepped into her structures, with the bishop of Rome and other bishops functioning as both civil as well as religious rulers. Bishops acted in much the same way as governors in Roman imperial provinces, especially where there was a weak official or no civil alternative. Certainly popes can't be faulted for taking steps to protect their own interests; the Church needed peace, prosperity, protection, and freedom to keep her theology clear and her officials independent. That the popes decided to ensure these situations by adopting the monarchical systems of other monarchies and feudal hierarchies is also not surprising. These worked for the secular world, after all, so why reinvent the proverbial wheel? Also, to compete with these other power centers and to avoid being swallowed by them, popes decided that the cultural context of medieval Europe demanded that Church officials be seen at least as the equal of civil officials, with theology providing the topper. The final authority on the planet must be the Church, since every official hoped to make his way to heaven.

However, there were also negative aspects of papal monarchy. With a bureaucracy staffed by fallible human beings, opportunities for corruption and bribery would not always be resistible. The Church could, and sometimes did, get so caught up in the pageantry and raw competition of power politics that she lost sight of her humble beginnings with Jesus. Some popes, cardinals, and bishops were less priestly and more secular than anyone would have liked, then or now. At times, too, the papacy reached too far and paid a price.

The worst example of a papacy losing a dangerous game led to the Avignon papacy. A very weak pope, Clement V (1305–1314), allowed himself to be swayed far too much by the French monarchy and transferred papal operations to southern France. Although there were valid reasons (mostly safety) for the papacy to make this move, the Avignon popes (all of whom were French) were slow to return home when the path was clear. What was supposed to be a short visit lasted nearly three-quarters of a century. Gregory XI (1370–1378) successfully returned to Rome, but his death shortly afterward led to more trouble—the Great Western Schism of 1378–1409. (The Great Western Schism is not the same thing as the so-called Great Schism, which refers to the simmering division between Greek East and Latin West that was formalized in 1054 and lifted in 1965.)

The Great Western Schism began with the 1378 conclave, which was deadlocked between a few Italians and the larger number of French cardinals eager to get back to Avignon. They settled on a compromise: an Italian archbishop with long experience in Avignon. Urban VI (1378–1389) acted so erratically that within a few months most of these cardinals declared his election invalid because of a riot that occurred outside the conclave. Led by the French, they elected one of their own, who became Clement VII (1378–1394), and soon went back to Avignon. Meanwhile, Urban VI (the Roman pope) and Clement VII (the Avignon pope) each created his own college of cardinals, excommunicated the other pope and his cardinals, and set up rival papacies.

Two lines of popes followed until 1409, when most of both colleges of cardinals had enough. They held a council at Pisa, deposed the Roman and Avignon popes, and elected what they hoped was a unifying pope known as the Pisan or conciliar pope. Neither of the other popes accepted the move, so now there were three popes and three colleges of cardinals—in essence, three papacies. Finally, a general council at Constance (1414–1418) accept-ed the Roman pope's resignation, deposed the Avignon and Pisan/conciliar pope, and got everyone to agree that whoever was elected would enjoy complete allegiance and obedience. After thirty-nine years, Martin V (1417–1431) unified the papacy and set about a process of restoring papal authority and prestige.

THE CHURCH IN THE PEWS

A fascinating aspect of medieval church history is that, while the papacy was becoming monarchical and some-times worldly, the Church as it lived in the pews practiced a lively, vibrant, and innovative spirituality that apparent-ly did not lose faith, even when the Church—the seamless garment of Christ—was split three ways. Maybe the most important path to this piety was the final disappearance of a persistent Arianism by the turn of the millennium. Recall that, early in the fourth century, Arius had said Jesus may have been a superhuman, but he wasn't quite divine. To counter that heresy, the Church emphasized Je-sus as God, often seen in artwork sitting sternly in judg-ment at the end of time. With Arianism gone, Christians could turn comfortably and safely to a more approachable Jesus. This rediscovery of Jesus as he appears in his daily life in the gospels—as opposed to the Jesus of technical theological language—is called an evangelical awakening and is the key to appreciating medieval spirituality.

Because the gospel Jesus was now the focus, Christians found in him a model of behavior for their own difficult lives of trying to hope in the face of fear, especially of death, which was often closer than in the modern world. The Middle Ages, after all, was a world without penicillin. Consequently, Christians could readily identify with the Jesus who wept, who ate with his friends, who was challenged by others, who struggled and prayed, and whose body bled and died. It is no surprise, then, that medieval artwork moved away from earlier themes to focus less on the glorified Christ than on the crucified Jesus. As a direct result of the fascination with Jesus' humanity, Christians also naturally focused on his mother, Mary, by looking at her steadfast faith, especially at the foot of the cross, which made Saturday "her" day each week. An attractive image was of Mary accepting God's plan in *pietà* portraits where she holds her son's dead body. Her own model of a life of prayer was popularized in rituals that became the rosary during the Middle Ages.

What else made up this piety and spirituality? There are several notable practices that coalesce around the theme of the approachable Jesus who saved believers through his suffering. The most obvious was a fascination with the very life of Jesus, starting with his birth in Bethlehem. Francis of Assisi (1181/2–1226) reconstructed a Nativity scene just so he could preach to an illiterate audience using visual cues common to everyone: a newborn's first night on earth. This was a Jesus that a peasant could embrace: poor, outcast, vulnerable. This famous scene was part of a broader attempt to imitate Christ—in Latin, the *imitatio Christi* tradition—in whatever way you could.

The imitation of Christ took several forms, many of which revolved around an apostolic life of service that recalled the very first decades and centuries of Christianity. It was an age of great fervor, even excessive emotion, in religious activities outside the Mass. Penance became a focus, especially during Lent, with the famous flagellants walking their penitential roads to atone publicly (though often anonymously in hoods) for their sins. This type of *vita apostolica* could be lived by both men and women; in addition, it was available to all in their daily lives. Spirituality, therefore, was moving away from (but not canceling out) the monastery and convent where monks and nuns withdrew from the world. Here was a world to be lived in and saved, as Jesus had done. Toward that end, medieval peasants could read (or, more frequently, hear) a gospel story and place themselves within that scene. They might do what Jesus had done and preached: feed the hungry, clothe the naked, care for the needy, help the hopeless—doing good through corporal works of mercy and charitable acts for the least of Jesus' brothers and sisters, just as he himself had said to do in Matthew's Gospel.

Because their own lives were so fragile, medieval Christians looked to Jesus' passion for consolation, knowing he had suffered, too. There are many medieval sermons and works of art about Jesus' fears in Gethsemane as well as his scourging and crucifixion, sometimes in grotesque detail. Holy Week was the highlight of the liturgical year, but the peasants' focus was more on Good Friday than Easter Sunday, since they could make an emotional link between Jesus' pain and their own. So we find a devotion to Jesus as the man of sorrows, as well as attempts to follow his path along what developed into the Stations of the

Cross, which was a practice brought back by pilgrims to the Holy Land—a movement of increasing popularity in the Middle Ages that was in itself an attempt to literally walk in the footsteps of Christ.

If pilgrims couldn't undertake the costly, lengthy, and frequently deadly journey to the Holy Land, they might visit the shrines of regional saints, or visit, venerate, or own relics of local saints. (Think of Chaucer's pilgrims telling tales on their way to Becket's tomb in Canterbury.) Increasingly in the Middle Ages, these saints were not models of martyrdom, as in the first millennium, but neighbors who did the best they could and who could more readily be imitated. They came to consist mainly of men but also more women, clergy but more laypeople, with a greater variety of ages and professions, and more in cities than in the countryside. They were celebrated in miracle and morality plays, in frequent festivals and feast days, and through local-dialect sermons that made direct and easy connections between a saint's exemplary life and the struggles of people in a specific region, profession, or state of life such as parenthood. Medieval spirituality also embraced the classic conflict embodied by the story of the sisters who were friends of Jesus, the everyday tension between Mary's contemplation and Martha's activity.

Eucharistic devotion rose, too, but not in terms of receiving Communion, which most people did only once a year, probably because of a sense of their own sinfulness and therefore reverence for Jesus as present in the consecrated host. The devotion to Jesus' broken body dovetailed with the Eucharist as the body of Christ *(corpus Christi).* Since Christians were not receiving the Eucharist physically, they worshiped Jesus from afar: by attending Mass and raising their eyes at the elevation of the host when bells were rung, by participating in processions and the equivalent of Forty Hours' devotions, and by receiving blessings pronounced over them by priests holding monstrances.

There was more to this *vita apostolica* than just devotional practices within the evangelical awakening. Because of the troubles with worldliness in the Church's hierarchy, spirituality in the Church's body acted sometimes as a check and other times as an outright critique. There were complaints that prelates had become distanced from the gospels' simplicity, poverty, humility, and purity; some had been tainted by worldliness. And, then as now, some critics with valid observations crossed the line. True, some of these members of what came to be called poor men's movements deserve credit for casting aside their wealth to more radically follow the gospel message. They lived the gospel with dynamism and personal witness as well as with a practical and spiritual bent.

We should note that the Franciscans and Dominicans are laudable examples of these movements. Theirs was a new type of religious order for a new urban context seething with evangelical emotion. The friars would be beggars *(mendicants)* in the world instead of monks who chose to pray in cloisters. Francis, for example, lived this evangelical awakening when he cast aside his father's wealth and embraced the gospels' *vita apostolica.* Unlike other preachers whom we will discuss in a moment, however, he always saw himself as a loyal son of the church. He did not believe he had a vocation to the priesthood, but he humbly agreed to be ordained a deacon because only with this official Church approval could he validly preach. He and his Franciscan followers encapsulated the evangelical awakening with a spirituality that was incarnational (like Jesus, they wanted to embrace and sanctify the world, not withdraw from it), ecclesial (in that they were obedient to Church authority), poor (as were Jesus and his followers), and evangelical (in embracing the gospels' purity in its essence). Francis' contemporary Dominic Guzman (1170–1221) embraced other aspects of the times. Similar to Francis, he was taken with the apostolic life and poverty, but unlike Francis, he embraced a more intellectual approach in tune with the scholastic humanism at work in the new universities. Dominic and his new order, the Dominicans, believed they must counter heresy through intellectual study and debate grounded in personal holiness.

And heresy there certainly was. Idealism and literalism can be both praiseworthy and troubling. Some within the poor men's movements adopted a holier-than-thou approach toward other peasants and the hierarchy, leading to the typical dangers of zealotry. In their attempt to champion the laity and criticize clerical excess, some became anticlerical themselves and grew so disgusted with the Church's hierarchy that they began to operate outside of it—for instance, by preaching without permission from the bishop. Here is where medieval heresy arose, not from misunderstanding complicated theological vocabulary of the first millennium, but from critiquing too harshly the institutional developments of the Middle Ages.

Ironically, many medieval heresies ended up creating their own parallel churches, sometimes on a very large scale. One group, the *Waldensians,* was started by a man very much like Francis who repudiated his family wealth and radically embraced poverty. Known colloquially as Peter Waldo, he died in 1205, putting him in the same generation as Francis and Dominic. Like Francis, Peter was at first looked upon with caution by Church authorities; unlike Francis, Peter resisted attempts to bring his movement within the Church's authority as it flourished in northern Italy, southeast Germany, Bohemia, and around Lyons in France. Waldensians eventually rejected the Church's sacraments, devotional customs and rituals, and structures, as did another heresy that was more widespread. The *Albigensians* were also known as the Cathars (or *Cathari:* "pure ones") and had roots in earlier heresies that rejected all matter as evil—which created obvious problems for Jesus' Incarnation, passion, and resurrection.

Now firmly established with her own court system and authority, the institutional Church could meet this challenge from within her own pews with the formal establishment of inquisitorial procedures begun by Popes Innocent III and Gregory IX in the early thirteenth century. Inquisitors, frequently the well-trained Dominicans, were directly under papal authority, since some bishops had not done as much as they could have to fight heresy in their dioceses. There was a formal process of inquisition. A period of inquiry was announced along with an immediate time of amnesty (typically a week to forty days), after which witnesses could come forward in procedures that strike us as lacking in due process: anonymous accusations, no chance to rebut witnesses, no legal representation, no protection from self-incrimination, and sometimes torture. (This first phase of inquisition was a bit different from the Spanish Inquisition, which was more an arm of the state and operated in the very late Middle Ages and during the Reformation.) So strong was the threat of heresy that Pope Innocent III in 1209 applied the privileges granted to Holy Land crusaders to those who fought Albigensians. Many historians now see this as a distortion of the crusading ideal, which leads us to the next section of our story of the medieval church.

WHAT MAKES THIS PERIOD UNIQUE?

The Crusades are another of those emblematic topics that spring to mind when someone says "the medieval church" or just "the Middle Ages." We have seen how the crusading effort was applied to fighting heretics within the Church, but that was a later development. We should look at the Crusades from multiple perspectives: their spiritual roots, their political and military aspects and events, and their impact.

First, the crusading movement is linked with pilgrimage in something of a chicken-and-egg relationship, since the Holy Land was the pilgrimage site par excellence. Church officials there and in Europe were concerned that Christians on their way to and from the area were being harassed—meaning robbed and at times killed—by

Muslims. The desire for pilgrimage and therefore crusade was a living part of medieval spirituality and the sentiments of the Church in the pews. There was a strong desire to get as close as possible to Jesus by visiting the earthly sites of his birth, life, ministry, death, and resurrection. Clearly, then, the physical path for pilgrims had to be cleared and protected, which leads us to the political and military side of the Crusades.

Fundamentally, the Crusades began as the attempt to protect Christians under Muslim rule, although this effectively meant recovering control of the Holy Land from Muslims, who had taken the area as part of their initial expansion in the seventh century. Europeans who promised to "take up the cross" (*crux*, in Latin) sewed a cross, typically of red fabric, on their clothing and shouted "God wills it!" *(Deus vult)* or "God's will!" Significantly, these military personnel enjoyed the same status as unarmed pilgrims and considered their Crusader's vow to have been fulfilled when they prayed at the site of the crucifixion and resurrection in the Church of the Holy Sepulchre.

Historians don't all agree on the numbering of the Crusades, but the first few are clear. The First Crusade occurred as a result of the speech of Pope Urban II in France in 1095, which is seen rightly as the inauguration of the crusading movement. He mentioned the need for pilgrims to be protected and may have been inspired by the Christians' defeat of the Muslims in Spain in 1085, which reminds us that Christians had been "crusading" in Spain since the eighth century when Muslims took over the Iberian Peninsula. We should note, too, that the

Christian reconquest of Spain had been proceeding since then and would not conclude until 1492.

The initial call for crusade was also a part of the papal revolution to stress the pope's authority over all of Christianity, both East and West. Urban II said he was responding to a request for aid from the Byzantine emperor in Constantinople, which would have served papal attempts at reasserting their authority in the East, particularly after 1054's mutual excommunications. Inspired by Urban II, this First Crusade was the only successful one in terms of taking Jerusalem, which the crusaders did in 1099 in a bloody massacre of Muslims.

After Muslims regained some territory, a Second Crusade followed in 1147–1149, and then a Third Crusade (1189–1192) responded to the Muslim recapture of Jerusalem in 1187, which replicated the massacre of 1099 but with Christians on the losing side this time. The Third Crusade allowed for safer passage for pilgrims, however, which benefited both traveling Christians and the Muslim tourist economy in the region. A Fourth Crusade (1198–1204) was an abominable mess in which European Christians, frustrated by their inability to make it to the Holy Land, turned their fury instead against their fellow Christians, the Greek-speaking Eastern Christians, and brutally sacked Constantinople. A Fifth Crusade (1213–1221) replicated the Third: although the leaders did not take Jerusalem, safe passage was arranged for pilgrims. Other smaller, less-organized crusades were sprinkled in and followed these five, but the movement had run the major part of its course by the late thirteenth century.

Apart from the obvious geopolitical impact of taking and losing Jerusalem while negotiating pilgrims' safety, the Crusades had a serious influence on relations among Jews, Christians, and Muslims—all of whom share a common ancestor in Abraham, are "children of the Book," and consider Jerusalem a sacred place. Medieval Muslims and Christians never did understand each other religiously and culturally, of course, though at times the sources indicate a certain admiration for each other's bravery. As a result of Christian attempts to retake Jerusalem, the city grew in stature within Islam, attracting literary and financial interest. More money was poured into its buildings, and the city became the object of poetry and of sayings celebrating its importance to Islam.

A lesser-known but no less serious part of the Crusades was how they harmed Jews. The logic, if it can be called that, ran this way: if Crusaders were going off to fight the unfaithful ones—the infidel (and we must recall that Muslims and Christians were "infidels" to each other)—far away in the Holy Land, what of non-Christians at home? In short, Jews in particular locations in Europe were massacred by Christian Crusaders on their way to the Holy Land as part of the effort to free Jesus' land from dirty hands—to view it in the worst terms. Indeed, a pogrom against Jews that was related to the Holy Land predated Urban II's speech by almost a century. In 1009, a Muslim caliph named Hakim ordered the destruction of the Church of the Holy Sepulchre. In France, some Christians decided that the Jews of their region had paid Hakim to do so, and they were forced to be baptized or were massacred in revenge. So, too, in 1096, Christians killed Jews in and around Speyer, Worms, Cologne, Mainz, and Prague on their way to Jerusalem. The same thing happened in the Rhineland with the Second Crusade half a century later.

This is the horrid and sad side of the story, and it cannot be denied. It is a reminder, too, of just how much Christianity controlled Western society. Indeed, part of what ultimately makes this period unique is that the Middle Ages is the era in which the Roman Catholic Church *was* European society. Often, the word *Christendom* is used to describe the age, but this is a word that connotes an institution and a heavy clamp of authority. A better word is a medieval Latin one, *Christianitas,* which cannot be translated because there is no English equivalent. Perhaps "Christianity-ness" will have to do as an ugly mouthful, but the point is that the Catholic Church was the very glue of European society. The medieval church exercised a religious, social, economic, political, and cultural leadership—even monopoly—that it would never replicate after the Reformation and Enlightenment to come.

DISCUSSION QUESTIONS

1. *Did anything about medieval church history surprise you?*

2. *Did anything about the medieval church strike you as particularly familiar?*

3. *What models and lessons might be drawn from the medieval church for today?*

4. *Do you think the papal revolution was a positive and/or negative development? Are there aspects that we should adopt? Are there aspects that are best left to the past?*

5. *Do you see any links between the medieval evangelical awakening and movements within the Church today?*

6. *What is the legacy of the Crusades for the world today?*

7. *Give a portrait of the medieval church to someone who knows nothing about it. What three main elements would you emphasize? Why?*

8. *When medieval Christians thought of the word* church, *what would they have had in mind?*

FURTHER READING

Hillgarth, J. N., ed. *Christianity and Paganism, 350–750: The Conversion of Western Europe*. Philadelphia: University of Pennsylvania Press, 1986.

Lynch, Joseph H. *The Medieval Church. A Brief History*. New York: Longman, 1992.

Miller, Maureen C. *Power and the Holy in the Age of the Investiture Conflict. A Brief History with Documents*. Boston: Bedford/St. Martin's, 2005.

Mollat, G. *The Popes at Avignon*. 9th ed. Translated by Janet Love. New York: Harper and Row, 1965.

Morris, Colin. *The Papal Monarchy: The Western Church from 1050 to 1250*. Oxford: Clarendon Press, 1989.

Oakley, Francis. *The Western Church in the Later Middle Ages*. Ithaca, NY: Cornell University Press, 1979.

Peters, Edward, ed. *Heresy and Authority in Medieval Europe*. Philadelphia: University of Pennsylvania Press, 1980.

Riley-Smith, Jonathan. *The Crusades. A Short History*. New Haven: Yale University Press, 1987.

Shinners, John, ed. *Medieval Popular Religion, 1000–1500. A Reader*. Ontario: Broadview Press, 1997.

Speed, Peter, ed. *Those Who Prayed*. New York: Italica Press, 1997.

Swanson, R. N. *Religion and Devotion in Europe, c. 1215–c. 1515*. Cambridge: Cambridge University Press, 1995.

Winston-Allen, Anne. *Stories of the Rose. The Making of the Rosary in the Middle Ages*. University Park, PA: Pennsylvania State University Press, 1997.

CHAPTER 3

The Reformation Church
(ca. 1500–1700)

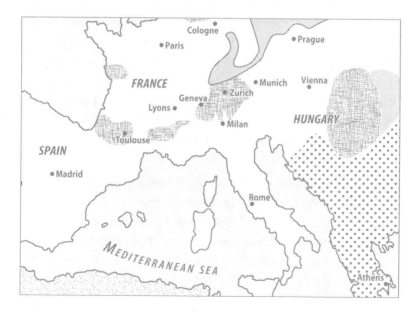

Timeline

ca. 1500	African slaves brought to Caribbean
1508–1512	Michelangelo paints Sistine Chapel ceiling
1509	Erasmus, Dutch reformer, points out Church problems in *Praise of Folly*
1512–1517	Fifth Lateran Council
1515–1582	Teresa of Ávila, Spanish mystic and reformer
1517	Martin Luther posts *95 Theses* on door of Wittenberg Cathedral
1509–1564	John Calvin, theologian and reformer
1519–1522	One of Magellan's ships is first vessel to sail around the world
1519–1521	Cortés conquers Aztecs in Mexico
1524	Verrazano explores New York Harbor
1532–1533	Pizarro conquers Incas in Peru
1534	England's Henry VIII establishes Church of England with himself as head
1540	Ignatius of Loyola's Society of Jesus founded
1542–1549	Francis Xavier, Jesuit missionary, in India and Japan
ca. 1545–1563	Council of Trent
1552–1610	Matteo Ricci, Jesuit missionary to China
1555	Peace of Augsburg settles Catholicism and Lutheranism as two dominant forms of Christianity in Europe
1564–1616	William Shakespeare
1588	Spanish Armada defeated by "Protestant Winds" and Queen Elizabeth I's navy off coast of England
1564–1642	Galileo, physicist and astronomer
1618–1648	Thirty Years' War between Protestant Union and Catholic League
1619	African slaves brought to America's Virginia colony
1620	*Mayflower* lands in New England
1687	Sir Isaac Newton publishes *Principia Mathematica,* a leading work of the Scientific Revolution
1688	England's Glorious Revolution establishes a constitutional monarchy

	CATHOLICS
	LUTHERANS
	REFORMED/CALVINISTS
	ANGLICANS
	ORTHODOX
	MUSLIM

ICELAND

NORTH ATLANTIC

NORWAY

Oslo

SWEDEN

Stockholm

•Edinburgh

Armagh•

York•

BALTIC SEA

DENMARK

Copenhagen•

London•
Canterbury•

Cologne•

POLAND

•Paris

•Prague

FRANCE

Munich•

Vienna•

Lyons•

Geneva• Zurich•

•Milan

HUNGARY

•Toulouse

PORTUGAL

SPAIN

•Madrid

•Lisbon

Rome•

MEDITERRANEAN SEA

Athens•

REFORMATION CHURCH, c. 1600

THE BIG PICTURE

As united as Christianity was in the Middle Ages, she become utterly divided in the Reformation that followed. The story of the Reformation is the story of how the words *Christianity* and *Roman Catholicism* came to be no longer synonymous. Before the early sixteenth century, it is redundant to refer to *Catholic Christianity*. At least in the West, to be Roman Catholic meant you were Christian and vice versa. After the early sixteenth century, we must always clarify: a Roman Catholic is still a Christian, but not every Christian is a Roman Catholic. What had been until this point in time a shared history became a parallel history, with the only points of intersection being conflict, not union.

We should begin by making the familiar statement that Martin Luther (1483–1546) did not set out to break away from the Church, to start a revolution, or to establish Protestantism. An Augustinian monk and Scripture scholar, Luther came from a monastic and university climate that was trying to reform the Church by rediscovering her roots. Luther looked back to the early church and saw an alleged golden age before Constantine created an imperial church. He considered his own time one of confusion needing reform. For Luther, what stood between the past and his own present was a millennium of medieval departures from the gospel's purity. His goal was simple: to move the Church forward by recovering her ancient glory. Others who followed Luther went even faster and further than he did, which makes a narrative approach the best way to see the big picture of the Reformation from the perspectives of Protestant alternatives to Catholic Christianity and the Catholic Church's responses.

When Luther posted his *95 Theses*—a list of observations—on the door of the Wittenberg Cathedral in 1517, he intended to offer fair criticisms of the way the Church was operating at the time and to spark a discussion of how to fix things. He was particularly upset by the sale of indulgences, which were related to the concept of the treasury of the saints. Since the saints were already in heaven, they had no need for the merits they garnered by their good deeds during their lives. Meanwhile, even after Christians on earth had confessed their sins, done penance, and received absolution, they still "owed time" in purgatory. Indulgences were a way to whittle that time down and were typically earned by doing corporal works of mercy, going on pilgrimage, or performing other spiritual acts of prayer or service. A trade in indulgences developed, whereby people could buy the indulgence without doing the good deed. Sometimes, that money was used for pious purposes, but Luther was disturbed because recently in his homeland of Germany a particularly notorious indulgence peddler named Tetzel was sending the money to Rome to build a new St. Peter's Basilica and to pay off the debts a German archbishop tallied up as he bribed his way to heading three dioceses—making him guilty of simony (buying an office), pluralism (holding more than one job), and therefore absenteeism (since he could only be at one of those jobs at any one time). For Luther, this was the worst example of a Church hierarchy that had become greedy, and of a spirituality that had become one of arithmetical piety and not genuine holiness.

Luther's criticisms took a sharp turn in 1520 when he issued three pamphlets that attacked an unworthy hierarchy as improperly political and instead asserted the priesthood of all believers. In addition, he recognized just three of the seven sacraments and held that human beings are saved (or "justified") by faith alone regardless of their good deeds. After famously standing his ground in an inquiry, Luther was excommunicated in 1521 and thereafter virulently opposed the papacy, sometimes in vile terms. Within a decade, the movement got its name when a number of secular rulers who opposed the pope more for political than religious reasons refused to enforce Luther's excommunication by protesting—hence the term "Protestant."

Lutheranism was only part of the movement that he unintentionally started. Another major branch followed John Calvin (1509–1564), who tried to literally reincarnate the earliest church with one in Geneva by having the church he led operate as closely to the New Testament model as possible—with pastors, teachers, elders, and deacons, but no popes, cardinals, or bishops because those words are not found in the gospels, The Acts of the Apostles, or epistles. Many Protestant groups took Calvin's organization—referred to as *Reformed Protestantism*—as a guide. Ironically, Calvin's Geneva was so organized and centralized that it came to be known as the Protestant Rome, with many Protestants coming to Geneva to learn his system, then returning to their home countries where they put their own version into practice. This process is how Protestantism itself splintered over the next decades and centuries into local churches, including Methodists, Presbyterians, Huguenots (French Calvinists), and quite a few others.

Many Protestant groups tried to set up theocracies in which ministers and magistrates were one and the same—not unlike Calvin's Geneva, in essence—and this organization reached across the Atlantic to some of the first communities in America. Although they were trying to recreate New Testament communities and offices, it is ironic that they ended up establishing churches in which religious authorities had civil power, which was one of their criticisms of bishops and popes at the time. Although some Protestant groups criticized Catholics for using condemnations and excommunications to get rid of their enemies, it was not uncommon for one Protestant group to condemn not only Catholics but other Protestants, even to the point of heresy trials and executions by burning.

More rigid groups quickly began to critique Luther and Calvin, saying they hadn't gone far enough, and these groups splintered from mainstream Protestantism in sometimes violent reactions not only to Catholicism, but to Lutheranism, as well. This movement is known as the *Radical Reformation* and is illustrated most clearly by the militant former Catholic priest Ulrich Zwingli (1484–1531), and then the Anabaptists who, in turn, challenged even Zwingli and had a bare-bones approach to church structure, liturgy, and practices. Radical groups had an apocalyptic (end-of-the-world) element, as well as believing that the final battles between good and evil were afoot. Like some believers in the first decades after Jesus, they expected his Second Coming imminently and so looked more to the Book of Revelation than The Acts of the Apostles as their guide. Some of the most ardent supporters of this strand of Protestantism took axes to organs, statues, and devotional objects.

Doctrinally, Protestants as a group generally reduced the seven Catholic sacraments to two or three. Some accepted baptism, and just adult baptism ("believer's baptism") at that, as the only sacrament. As far as the Eucharist was concerned, Protestants to varying degrees rejected the Catholic teaching of *transubstantiation* that describes how Jesus is really present as body and blood, with bread and wine only seeming to remain to human eyes, in a true sacrifice. Some took the idea a step down, using the word *consubstantiation* to say that the body and blood coexisted with the bread and wine, but remained only as long as the community was gathered together. Still others called the act the *Lord's Supper,* instead, to emphasize their belief that bread and wine remained to represent Jesus' body and blood, but a transformation of existence or coexistence never occurred, making the action symbolic or a memorial alone.

In England's special case, because of the desire of King Henry VIII (r. 1509–1547) for a male heir, he famously ran through six wives, splitting with his first wife and the Catholic Church because he couldn't get an annulment. The English Reformation was unique and quite a seesaw ride. Like the reform movements on the European continent, Henry VIII's efforts were fueled by a combination of religion, politics, and a growing nationalism. Unlike them, Henry VIII's changes were not very theological. Although the English king with Parliament created the Church of England (Anglicans in United Kingdom–affiliated countries and Episcopalians elsewhere) and declared the monarch as its head, under Henry the church's theology was largely still Catholic. Henry VIII kept seven sacraments along with clerical celibacy, Mary and the saints, transubstantiation, and infant baptism. Reformers more in line with aspects of Protestant theology had to wait for Henry VIII's son, Edward VI (r. 1547–1553), whose youth allowed them to turn the Church of England more toward Protestantism. His short reign was followed by a Catholic restoration under Mary I (r. 1553–1558). In all of these switches back and forth, plenty of martyrs were made on both sides, such as Thomas More ("The king's good servant, but God's first.") under Henry, and Thomas Cranmer under Mary.

It was during the long, stabilizing reign of Elizabeth I (r. 1558–1603) that the Church of England became ever more Protestant in form and content, but still with an English twist. Elizabeth's path was an interesting middle way between Roman Catholicism, with what she considered its unacceptable papal dominance, and Protestantism, which was a bit too egalitarian and denominational for the queen and her bishops. It is notable, for instance, that the *Thirty-Nine Articles* of 1563 reads as much like a rejection of Roman Catholic ideas as it does of Anabaptist beliefs. And, of course, there is that particular English element of having the monarch also serve as the church's head. Still, even this middle ground was rejected as rather "popish" for the Puritans who, in the tradition of reforming reformers on the continent, split from the Church of England and became the American pilgrims of Plymouth Rock.

What of Roman Catholicism during this period? As we might expect, reactions ranged from reticent—Pope Leo X (1513–1521) dismissed Luther's *95 Theses* as a quarrel among monks—to self-reflective. Many Catholic reformers joined the more responsive Protestant ranks while others chose to stick with the Catholic Church and try to help her from within. Early in the struggle, Pope Adrian VI (1522–1523) instructed his delegate to a conference with Lutheran-leaning German princes to say flatly that the Church admitted many mistakes, starting at the very top. Pope Paul III (1534–1549) called in reformers from outside Rome to look at the situation, especially in the Curia, with fresh eyes. This team produced a strongly worded memo that specifically targeted the Roman bureaucracy and simony that ran through the Church's entire body. The memo recommended many reforms, including some touching on the training and examination of candidates for priesthood. It also recommended that bishops live in their dioceses, pushing back against pluralism and absenteeism, and that the sale of indulgences be closely regulated, which must have pleased Luther. But not every pope shared the perspective of Adrian VI and Paul III. A few years later, Paul IV (1555–1559) took just the opposite approach; he was closed to conversation about reform within Catholicism, let alone conversation with Protestants, and was largely reactionary, quite conservative, and rigid with all of his opponents.

Nevertheless, it was clear that the Roman Catholic Church had to respond to the Protestant criticisms. A general council was the best way to do so, but for a variety of reasons—including the fact that the Protestants were calling for one, too—popes and bishops held off for nearly three decades after Luther's *95 Theses*. The Catholic Council of Trent met in three acts: 1545–1548, 1551–1552, and 1562–1563. Between each session, a great deal of work was done, as well, making it an almost twenty-year period of concentrated effort.

Viewing the final product of all of the council's documents, we can see that the Church tried to face the major questions raised by the Protestants. The council, under strong papal direction, first stressed that the Church's authority was based not just on Scripture, as many Protestants were holding, but also on a living and ongoing tradition composed of actions, statements, and decisions made by popes, bishops, councils, and the early church fathers. Trent stressed that individual Christians could not authoritatively read and interpret the Bible on their own. The council reminded bishops of their roles as preachers, teachers, and decision-makers, while noting the need for an ordained, celibate clergy set apart from the laity instead of a Protestant priesthood of all believers based only on baptism.

Turning particularly to doctrine, once again the Council of Trent clarified Catholic positions against those of Protestants. Good works were indeed needed along with faith to get to heaven. The number of sacraments was reiterated at seven. Eucharist was clearly explained as including the Real Presence of Jesus. Reforms were put in place to improve the quality of priests and bishops, which led the council to introduce legislation creating seminaries as a formal school system. Familiar aspects of piety were retained, including relics and indulgences, but Catholics were cautioned against simply doing things superstitiously or in a misguided attempt to buy their way into heaven. It seemed, then, that some Catholics had been listening both to their own critics within as well as to some Protestants, now unfortunately outside what had ceased to be one united church.

THE CHURCH'S HIERARCHY

These were rough centuries for the Church's popes and bishops, but we must admit—as Pope Adrian VI had done—that some of the problems were of the Church's own making. During the fourteenth-century stay in Avignon, the Curia had largely turned into a bloated bureaucracy of small-minded officials, piles of costly paperwork, and complex levels of procedural minutiae, all of which translated into plenty of opportunities for bribery and a mentality that stopped valuing pastoral service and instead favored ambition and greed.

The nearly four decades of the Great Western Schism that followed the Avignon years severely damaged the papacy's prestige in both religious as well as political leadership. While there was some papal recovery in the fifteenth century, the Protestant charges against a political papacy—charges at times based in reality, even if related in vicious, offensive language—stalled those efforts in the early sixteenth century. Before and then especially after the Council of Trent, the papacy needed several decades to find its footing. For the papacy, the Reformation centuries may have been one of the worst times in its existence.

Renaissance and Reformation popes spent much of these centuries trying to restore their lost reputation in a number of ways: theologically, politically, and visually. Theologically, popes took control of the Church's general councils, which had become a bit more independent as a result of the Great Western Schism. Lateran V (1512–1517), under the feisty and worldly popes Julius II (1503–1513) and Leo X, pushed back against the ideas that a general council held power over a pope and that a pope did not have the authority to name bishops. Lateran V met in Rome, recalling the first four Lateran Councils of the Middle Ages, which had been decidedly papal events with bishops doing not much more than ratifying decisions the pope had already made. Fifteen- and sixteenth-century popes also reached agreements with Christians living in the East as a way of exercising—and pointing out their authority to exercise—their role as head and representative of Catholicism. Likewise, popes signed political concordats and treaties with secular rulers, placing themselves at least on an even plane with those rulers and once again demonstrating that the pope, and not a general council, was the highest authority in the Church when it came to religious and civil matters.

Finally, popes invested money in rebuilding and adorning Rome in a way that made it clear to everyone that this city, where Peter had been martyred, was the center of the Catholic world, and that Peter's successor, the pope, sat on the only throne that mattered. These popes, similar to many aristocrats in Europe but especially in Italy, acted as patrons of the arts who allowed literal Renaissance men such as Leonardo da Vinci (1452–1519) and Michelangelo (1475–1564) to devote their lives to painting, sculpting, and designing buildings—so many of which had religious themes. It was a period full of the iconography of power, and the source of that power was Jesus through Peter. The building of a new St. Peter's Basilica, which had contributed to Luther's disgust since indulgence money was partially footing the huge construction bill, was the centerpiece. Building continued for decades, stretching into centuries, until Pope Urban VIII finally consecrated the basilica in 1626. If the structure's majesty wasn't clear enough, the architect Bernini (1598–1680) added an imposing semicircle of columns outside the church to surround the piazza and to draw a believer inside, an elaborate "canopy" over the high altar that sat above Peter's tomb, and a monumental ceremonial throne of Peter behind it. Throughout Europe and then the "New World," a similar baroque architecture of power focused the eye clearly on Catholic centers of devotion and power in each church: the altar, the tabernacle, and the bishop's seat of authority.

Bishops worked closely with popes in implementing Trent as a top-down strategy of reform. Although Trent was closely controlled by several popes, it was also an episcopal event in that bishops played a large role in drafting and discussing the council's statements and decisions. Coming out of Trent, the bishops acted as the connection—the neck—between the Church's head and her body. Surprising to some is the fact that, while the late Middle Ages leading up to the Reformation were mostly a low point as far as the quality of bishops was concerned, the decades and centuries after the Council of Trent witnessed many energetic, faithful, farsighted, honest, and holy bishops who worked hard to recover Catholicism from the blows it had received from Protestant critics, to get the Catholic Church back on track, and to push her forward in a world that had instantly doubled in size when Columbus sailed from Spain in 1492.

This was an age of popes and bishops who were administrators and canon lawyers more than spiritual visionaries and theologians. The Church's hierarchy, dominated by these organizer popes and bishops, tried to maintain oversight of Trent's implementation by issuing documents, decisions, and publications from Rome in the late sixteenth century. Any questions raised by Trent's wording had to be channeled back to Rome for an authoritative interpretation. Within a few decades, Rome's popes, bishops, theologians, liturgists, Scripture scholars, and curialists published a new breviary (a book of the priest's prayers), missal (to guide Mass, sacraments, and other rituals), a profession of faith (that made clear what Catholics believed—and therefore where Protestants didn't agree), and a fresh version of the Bible, albeit still in Latin unlike the Protestant vernacular translations, starting with Luther's everyday German. The Curia was reorganized as well to streamline operations and bring them under greater papal and episcopal control. Although they were slow to follow Luther's lead, popes and bishops eventually embraced the printing press to spread catechetical materials and other Church documents guiding reform.

The poster child for the reforming bishop is the well-known example of Carlo Borromeo (1538–1584), the archbishop of Milan. True, Borromeo was the nephew of a pope and had received his red hat not long after his teenage years, but he was also a genuine reformer and spiritual pastoral leader. Though only twenty-seven when he arrived in Milan, he knew Trent's program well since he had been involved in many of the discussions concerning how to reform liturgy, sacraments, and the education of priests and the laity. He dressed as a bishop, not a cardinal, and placed himself at the service of his fellow bishops and priests in his own dioceses and elsewhere, often gathering them to listen to their concerns and then to offer direction and advice. Borromeo also centralized and streamlined his diocesan administration as Rome's Curia had done while opposing pluralism and absenteeism. Throughout Catholic territories, bishops were instructed to live in their dioceses and to hold only one pastoral office at a time. Buying and selling Church offices, always illegal but often permitted, was abolished and patrolled more effectively. Reaching back to early church procedures, bishops were to gather their priests annually and to meet with their own archbishop once every three years. Bishops were to maintain close ties with Rome, too, by visiting at regular intervals of three to ten years (based on location) and by sending reports of their synods and decisions to Rome. The goal was to make sure that a reformed Catholicism was operating uniformly at all levels, starting with the Church's head and moving down to her pews.

THE CHURCH IN THE PEWS

The Reformation was as much a social, cultural, and political phenomenon as it was a religious event. Historians trying to find the cause-and-effect often end up tangled in the proverbial question, "Which came first: the chicken or the egg?" Certainly there was discontent among Catholics in the pews against worldly bishops and priests who were disconnected from their peasant lives of struggle and poverty. Luther's theological discontent would have fueled that kind of criticism, but we must remember that Luther, Calvin, and the others in the vanguard of the Protestant Reformation were often theologians making careful and precise distinctions among complex aspects of philosophy and theology. This is not to say that the people in the pews were stupid, only that their faith—as we saw in chapter 2—operated largely on a much more visceral, emotional, tangible level as they tried to connect with a Jesus who was like them. Yes, popes, cardinals, and bishops were the

Church's prelates and they stood in need of criticism and correction, but very few Christians in the pews even knew who the pope was.

Something similar to what occurred in the Middle Ages was repeated during the Reformation era. While battles raged above them in the Church's hierarchy and in the highest echelons of university and political life, the people in the pews largely continued to exercise their faith mostly unchecked until decades after the Council of Trent. This fact causes both admiration and concern.

First, admiration. We should not fail to note that the people in the pews—both Protestant and Catholic—held onto their faith even though they were living through a time of confusion, challenge, reorganization, and the introduction of new alternatives. On the Catholic side, for example, we may have an English portrait of a faith holding strong under attack. Some historians believe that the story of the English Reformation demonstrates how traditional Catholic piety resisted the changes of Henry VIII and his successors, which contradicts a prevailing narrative that had English parishioners singing the praises of their Anglican rescue from Catholic superstition. On the other side, many Protestants struggled to maintain their beliefs under Catholic assault. For all Christians, though they were sadly splintered and opposed to each other, this was an age of faith, not atheism; of fierce choices to remain Catholic or Protestant even in the face of martyrdom; and of discussions everywhere about key elements of Christian belief.

Second, concern. At the same time, we must admit

that the sometimes-superstitious piety that troubled Luther was largely untouched, and uncorrected, during the first few decades of tumult in the sixteenth century. There were Catholic critics within—and we think most especially here of Erasmus (ca. 1467–1536), an almost exact contemporary of Luther who, unlike the German monk, chose to stay inside the Church and to try to reform her that way. Erasmus saw it all coming. He had been publicly complaining about empty actions during the same years that Luther was getting clear in his own head what he thought was wrong with some Catholic practices. In 1503, Erasmus published a handbook of advice for Christians that advised avoiding sterile scholasticism that had lost its humanistic roots and embracing a plain, simple spirituality that was geared toward an individual's relationship with Jesus, genuine piety, and practical devotional actions that exercised a person's faith rather than totaled up indulgences in a balance-sheet mentality aimed at making the path to heaven shorter.

Like Luther, Erasmus feared that Christians, even the most well-intentioned among them, were spending too much time on the "what" of religious practices, such as venerating relics or statues of saints, going on pilgrimages, acting in or attending morality plays, or saying many prayers rapidly to multiply a good result—what we call *arithmetical piety*. Erasmus and Luther aimed to refocus Christians on the "why" of their faith, often by suggesting a believer substitute one good action or intention for a pile of rote prayers. Also like Luther, and following in the tradition of the medieval-evangelical awakening of which both were heirs, Erasmus wanted people to reconnect with the Scriptures, the Church's fathers, and early church practices as directly as possible. His sharp tongue, however, often got Erasmus into trouble, such as with the biting satires of worldly prelates, silly rituals, and egghead academics that appear in his *Praise of Folly*. Some Catholics didn't know whose side Erasmus was on, but he finally came out hard against some of Luther's teachings. So close were some of his opinions to parts of the Lutheran critique, at least at first, that a popular phrase declared Luther hatched the egg that Erasmus had laid.

What were these practices in the pews? Early Reformation Catholics were much like their medieval predecessors. Their faith was largely unsophisticated, but fervent. Their activities took place outside the context of the Mass more so than inside a church on Sunday mornings. There were eucharistic devotions such as processions and adoration that did not involve receiving Communion, attending and performing in miracle and morality plays, devotions to saints and their relics, and pilgrimages to nearby sites such as a local saint's tomb or to major destinations as far away as Santiago de Compostela in Spain and the Holy Land.

What the Protestant Reformation criticisms pointed out was just what reformers like the medieval Waldensians and, more recently, Erasmus had been saying: the fundamental belief behind arithmetical piety needed to be uncovered, polished, and refocused. When Luther and some other Protestant reformers saw what Catholics had been doing with relics, indulgences, and other pious activities—that is, trying to get through as many as possible as quickly as possible—they threw the proverbial baby out with the bath water. Many mainstream Catholic reformers, on the other hand, believed that most Catholic devotions should be retained, but that they clearly needed a tune-up. The Council of Trent, for example, abolished alms collectors, which was the job Luther's foil Tetzel had held. Although Trent affirmed what indulgences were all about, new regulations stipulated that they should be used properly for spiritual and not financial gain. So, too, did Trent allow Catholics to venerate relics, use icons and images, pray to the saints for intercession with God, and believe in miracles, but the Catholic Church after Trent supervised these devotional items and practices more closely.

The refocusing of Catholic spirituality in the pews after Trent typically centered on beliefs and practices that Protestants had questioned, changed, or exiled. Reformation Catholicism retained veneration of Mary, since some Protestants had charged Catholicism with idolatry as far as she is concerned. Mary was an attractive way to bind Catholics together everywhere, as opposed to the more decentralized Protestant churches multiplying throughout the sixteenth and seventeenth centuries. Because Mary was assumed into heaven and was not tied to any one place, she became a universal example for Christians everywhere and a kind of saint without a country. This was also true of saints connected to Mary, such as her husband Joseph and mother Anne.

Another example was the Eucharist, which Trent had explained carefully by reiterating the Real (and enduring) Presence through transubstantiation. Consequently, tabernacles within churches replaced outdoor processions to some degree, and single altars captured the attention of everyone in the largest urban churches instead of the many—and at times distracting—side altars of medieval Gothic cathedrals where multiple Masses were said simultaneously. Reception of the Eucharist probably rose from once a year to as many as four times each year for the average person, with aristocrats and royalty receiving perhaps monthly. While Protestants generally de-emphasized individual confession of sins, Catholics responded by focusing attention on how to confess sins and to receive absolution properly and more frequently, often as a precursor to receiving Communion.

Finally, we see an increase in religious instruction at the grassroots level. Catholic leaders around the time of Trent realized that Protestant and Catholic reformers had been onto something when it came to the understanding of the faith in parishes. Because religious instruction was poor, medieval people were apt to follow legend, rumor, and superstition as religious fact and theological truth. Since most Catholics were not grounded in their faith, the Protestant critiques seemed all the more plausible because Catholics didn't know their Bible and doctrines. This is one reason why one of the first documents to follow Trent was a catechism.

We turn to two new religious orders, the Ursulines and the Jesuits, to make this point. Religious orders are sometimes located, in people's minds, in the hierarchy, but most religious orders, and these two in particular, began to meet the needs of the average Catholic man, woman, and child. When Angela Merici (1474–1540) established what became the Ursulines, she had to fight against a trend to make sure nuns stayed behind convent walls. She saw the charism of her companions as being out among the people. They focused on teaching women and girls, especially widows, orphans, the poor, the ill, and reformed prostitutes. The plan was simple: if you train girls and women in the faith, when they become mothers they will be ready to act as their children's first teachers in the faith. If you train women, the Ursulines believed, you build the domestic Church and therefore the universal Church from the ground up. Among the several initiatives of Ignatius Loyola (1491–1556) and his first companions who became the Jesuits, educating elite boys stood out. While this might not fit into the emphasis of the Church recovering and flourishing in her pews, Ignatius believed that these elites would be leaders to set good examples for those throughout the social strata within which Catholicism still operated.

WHAT MAKES THIS PERIOD UNIQUE?

The period overlapping the late Middle Ages and the Reformation was a lively era of critique and debate. Still, we cannot deny that a major aspect of this period's uniqueness is fragmentation. For a millennium, Roman Catholic Christianity dominated Western Europe. After Luther, the Roman Catholic Church was no longer the only choice available to Christians. (We are excluding here the split between Latin West and Greek East, which was noted several times already.)

The first phase of this fragmentation in Western Europe was, as we've seen, Luther's initial criticisms of the Catholic Church in 1517. By 1520, Luther and the pope had parted company, although Luther and Erasmus remained in tense dialogue for about five more years. In 1530, Philip Melanchthon (1497–1560) gave Lutheranism a formal statement of belief with his *Augsburg Confession*. Some Protestants and Catholics tried twice in the 1540s to reconcile their differences, but the paired issues of justification and salvation remained insolvable when Lutheran and Catholic leaders rejected a middle way of talking about these key topics.

The Peace of Augsburg in 1555 marks a culmination of this first phase of fragmentation. This treaty did not explicitly invoke the famous Latin phrase attributed to it— *cuius regio, eius religio* ("whose region, his religion")— but the treaty effectively cracked Catholicism's monopoly at the same time that it marked the subjugation of religion as the glue of European society to politics. A political leader, not a religious leader, would decide what form of Christianity was acceptable in his region. But we should emphasize that, in 1555, the two major choices were either Catholicism or Lutheranism, since Calvinism was still largely confined to Geneva at this point.

The second phase, however, did not take long to settle in, as some of Luther's followers went further than he did or took his ideas in other directions. So we have Calvin with his major branch of Protestantism followed by those Protestants who set up a type of Calvinism attuned to their local cultures and areas. But fragmentation followed here, too: Zwingli emerged with the Anabaptists, the English Puritans appeared in response to what they saw as an Anglican state religion akin to Catholicism's hierarchy, and smaller groups set up their own churches— all trying to reform the various versions of the Protestant Reformation.

During the late 1500s and through the 1600s, the map of Catholic Europe was shattered. Some regions switched back and forth between Catholicism and some form of Protestantism. Parts of France, for instance, shuttled between Huguenots and Catholics during the several decades of the Wars of Religion. Ruling families fought a civil war with religion becoming just a plaything, making France a turf battle between French Catholics and Huguenots who slaughtered each other regularly as heretics. The Saint Bartholomew's Day Massacre in 1572 saw Catholics murdering about three thousand Protestants; thousands of Catholics were killed in the fighting, too. Ironically, all had arrived for a royal wedding between a Protestant groom and a Catholic bride intended to keep the peace. By the time that same groom, Henry IV, got to the French throne in 1594, he'd switched so many times it was hard for anyone, least of all himself, to know what he really believed in terms of religious allegiance—a waffling summed up best (or worst) by his claim that "Paris is worth a Mass."

Meanwhile, central Europe's Holy Roman Empire also witnessed the equivalent of wars of religion. An unsteady truce lasted from the Peace of Augsburg in 1555 until 1618, when the Thirty Years War erupted between a Protestant Union and the Catholic League. Other countries lined up on either side of what began mostly as a German conflict: the Danes and Swedes, for instance, joined Protestant German princes, many of whom fought Catholicism because of the power of the German prince-bishops, with an emphasis on opposing the prince side of the equation. Meanwhile, Catholic Spain and France helped the Catholic League—though these two Catholic countries were themselves competing with each other at the same time in an attempt to be the preeminent royal protectors of Catholicism in the line of Constantine and Charlemagne. Spain's "most Catholic king," Philip II (1556–1598), after all, had sent his Spanish Armada to pull England back into the Catholic fold, but the famed "Protestant winds" destroyed his fleet in 1588.

In 1648, the Peace of Westphalia added Calvinism as a choice for rulers who were able to regulate religion in their spheres of influence. Although a ruler was not allowed to impose his religion on individual believers, he could regulate public but not private worship, which gave a measure of toleration to Catholics in Protestant regions and Protestants in Catholic territories. The point to remember in this very confusing period is that the Christian religion had become a junior partner in battles for power that often had more to do with political, social, economic, cultural, and nationalistic competition than with religious allegiance, theological orthodoxy, and devotional piety. This is not to say that political leaders did not believe in Jesus, but it is fair to note that religion wasn't the only or even the highest item on their agendas. Still, saying

"God is on my side" is a powerful motivation to wipe out an enemy who challenges not only your faith, but your economic well-being, political prosperity, and territorial security.

Although this period is unique for its fragmentation and blood, another theme stands out, as well, and that is the multiplicity of religious reform ideas that were floating around during these centuries. A good way to understand this period's uniqueness is not to talk about one "Reformation" with a capital *R*, but to explore many reformations—with a deliberate lower-case *r,* and with an *s* at the end making it plural. Viewing the period through this lens, a few characteristics emerge. There was not just one Protestant Reformation, but a variety of reformations that became Protestant. Some of these Protestant reformations agreed with Luther in whole or part, but others deviated from him. Most of these reformations had early, middle, and later periods of development.

At the same time, there were Catholic reformations— again: little *r* and a plural *s*—that came before and after Luther, although admittedly the ones that attempted to correct the Catholic Church before Luther showed up did not have much success. As with the Protestant reformations, there were phases and varieties of the Catholic reformations that have been assigned different titles, not all of which are entirely accurate. To speak only of a *Catholic Reformation,* for instance, might overlook the fact that Roman Catholicism really didn't get serious about reform in a systematic way until after Luther. In an effort to display a continuity of reform, advocates of this phrase might (intentionally or not) want to portray a church that was fully self-aware of what was happening and would have straightened things out even without Luther—a dubious assumption. But, to speak exclusively of a *Counter-Reformation* that emphasizes discontinuity with the past and highlights reaction to Luther similarly ignores any honest critiques and efforts that were in the works before the *95 Theses*.

Another phrase sometimes used to describe the Catholic side of the story is *Tridentine Reformation,* referring to the aftermath of the Council of Trent. The problem with this phrase is that it is, itself, a caricature of a siege mentality that certainly did not follow Trent. Recent research demonstrates that, while the decades after Trent did follow a certain centralizing tendency, at least in the pews it was not an era of lockstep Catholicism devoid of vibrancy and some variety. This alleged siege mentality, in which the Church holed up behind tall walls and completely rejected the world, did not occur in such a way. True, the Church did resist some aspects of the Scientific Revolution, the Enlightenment, and political revolutions that tried to place power in the hands of the people instead of monarchs, but these were later developments that we will follow in the story of the modern church. A helpful phrase may be *early modern Catholicism,* used to describe the centralizing tendencies of Trent in addition to a period of missionary activity and growth beyond Europe. Although a short-term view might say Catholic Church history was on a downward spiral because of the Reformation era, a long-term view would find that, despite its

DISCUSSION QUESTIONS

1. *Did anything about Reformation church history surprise you?*

2. *Did anything about the Reformation church strike you as particularly familiar?*

3. *What models and lessons might be drawn from the Reformation church for today?*

4. *How do you think today's Catholics should view Luther, Calvin, and the other Protestant reformers of the sixteenth century?*

5. *How do you think today's Protestants should view Erasmus and other Catholic reformers of the sixteenth century?*

6. *Do you think that Protestants and Catholics have more similarities or differences—then and now?*

7. *Do you see any links and/or differences between the early church and the Reformation church?*

8. *Give a portrait of the Reformation church to someone who knows nothing about it. What three main elements would you emphasize? Why?*

9. *When Reformation Catholics and Protestants thought of the word* church, *what would they have had in mind?*

10. *When Reformation Catholics and Protestants thought of the word* reform, *what would they have had in mind?*

FURTHER READING

Bireley, Robert. *The Refashioning of Catholicism, 1450–1770: A Reassessment of the Counter Reformation.* Washington, DC: The Catholic University of America Press, 1999.

Bouwsma, William J. *John Calvin: A Sixteenth-Century Portrait.* New York: Oxford University Press, 1988.

Duffy, Eamon. *The Stripping of the Altars: Traditional Religion in England c. 1400–c. 1580.* New Haven: Yale University Press, 1992.

Lindberg, Carter. *The European Reformations.* Oxford: Blackwell, 1996.

Lindberg, Carter, ed. *The European Reformations Sourcebook.* Oxford: Blackwell, 2000.

Luebke, David M., ed. *The Counter-Reformation.* Oxford: Blackwell, 1999.

MacCulloch, Diamaid. *The Reformation: A History.* New York: Viking, 2004.

Oberman, Heiko. *Luther. Man Between God and the Devil.* Translated by Eileen Walliser-Schwarzbart. New Haven: Yale University Press, 1989.

Olin, John C., ed. *Catholic Reform. From Cardinal Ximenes to the Council of Trent 1495–1563.* New York: Fordham University Press, 1990.

O'Malley, John W. *Trent and All That: Renaming Catholicism in the Early Modern Era.* Cambridge, MA: Harvard University Press, 2000.

Tracy, James D. *Erasmus of the Low Countries.* Berkeley: University of California Press, 1996.

CHAPTER 4

The Modern Church
(ca. 1700-today)

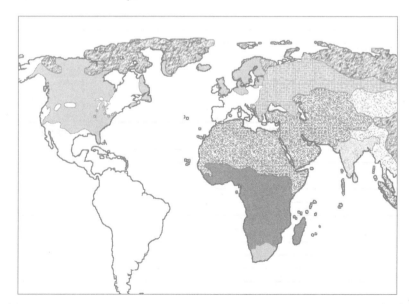

Timeline

1703–1791	John Wesley, founder of Methodism
1729–1796	Catherine the Great, tsarina of Russia
1776	American *Declaration of Independence*
1789	French Revolution begins; John Carroll elected first American bishop
1815	Napoleon's final defeat at Waterloo
1856–1939	Sigmund Freud, Austrian psychoanalyst
1859	Charles Darwin publishes *Origin of Species*
1861–1865	American Civil War
1863	Abraham Lincoln's *Emancipation Proclamation*
1867	Karl Marx publishes *Das Kapital*
1869–1870	First Vatican Council
1880	Thomas Edison patents the light bulb
1883	Pope Leo XIII opens the Vatican Archives
1905	Albert Einstein publishes four essays laying out his theory of relativity
1914–1918	World War I
1917	Russian Revolution
1939–1945	World War II and the Holocaust
1940s–1970s	European colonies in Asia, Africa, Oceania, and Caribbean gain political independence and governmental self-sovereignty
1948	United Nations' *Universal Declaration of Human Rights*
1962–1965	Second Vatican Council
1963	Martin Luther King, Jr. delivers his "I Have a Dream" speech
	President John F. Kennedy assassinated
1969	Astronaut Neil Armstrong walks on the moon
1978	Karol Wojtyla elected first non-Italian pope since 1523
1989	Berlin Wall falls

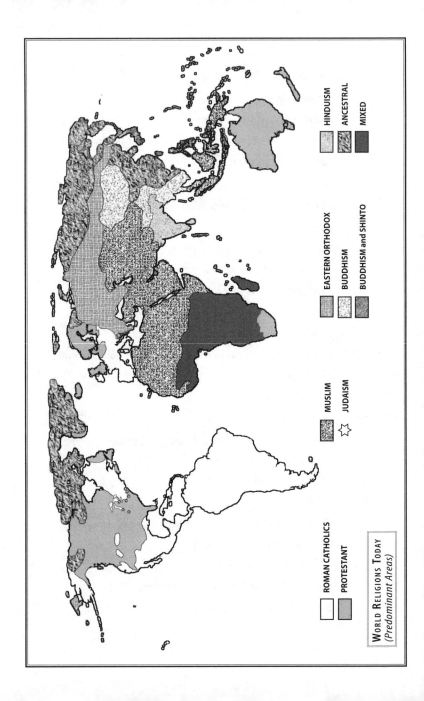

WORLD RELIGIONS TODAY
(Predominant Areas)

ROMAN CATHOLICS

PROTESTANT

MUSLIM

JUDAISM

EASTERN ORTHODOX

BUDDHISM

BUDDHISM and SHINTO

HINDUISM

ANCESTRAL

MIXED

THE BIG PICTURE

If you can remember the first time you put on a pair of sunglasses, or the last time you filled a new prescription for glasses and experienced that moment of, "Wow! Everything looks different," then you can understand how the Scientific Revolution and Enlightenment changed the way people saw the world. It was as if everyone got a new prescription and started to look around with a changed perspective— and then began to reflect on the ways they used to look at things and rethink those ways, too. The histories of the Scientific Revolution and the Enlightenment are complex. We will go into just some detail here to indicate the extent of the impact of these new ways of thinking not only on Catholicism, but also on the very idea of religious faith in a world growing daily more advanced in science, technology, secularism, and political participation.

The story begins a bit before our shorthand 1700 starting date for modernity with the Scientific Revolution that was the launching pad for the Enlightenment. Both relied on scientific methodology and human rationalism to an unprecedented extent that frequently overlooked or even demeaned the concept of revealed religious truth, although not every scientist or philosopher was an atheist. The best-known Scientific Revolution episode as far as church history is concerned involves the solar system. The Polish astronomer Copernicus (1473–1543) figured out that the Sun, and not the Earth, must be at the center of our system of planets. Galileo (1564–1642), using his own more sophisticated telescope, proved Copernicus' theory to be scientific fact, which caused him to run into trouble with his friend and one-time defender, now Pope Urban VIII (1623–1644). Switching from a geocentric (Earth-centered) to a heliocentric (Sun-centered) model influenced not only science and math, but religion and philosophy as well, since it took the Earth—and Jerusalem, commonly seen as the center of the Earth on medieval maps—out of the central position.

When it comes to modernity, you can't glibly declare, "This led to that." That said, it seems true that once the Earth was out of its privileged position, other long-held beliefs came under scrutiny, too. To be fair, what seemed to be happening was that authority itself had come under suspicion, challenge, and even assault. Examples are kings being toppled in England and France, Catholicism's monopoly being questioned first by Luther and then many others, and long-held beliefs in religion and science undergoing close scrutiny. The movements can be summed up with a word—*liberalism*—that has little to do with current politics and everything to do with its Latin root meaning freedom, as in "liberty."

Enlightenment liberalism does not mean FDR's New

Deal in the 1930s or LBJ's Great Society in the 1960s. In its own context, Enlightenment liberalism indicated freedoms that blossomed in the American Bill of Rights: the liberty to speak, to meet, to write, to protest, to practice any religion, and to be unrestricted in the exercise of civil liberties grounded in natural law. No question seemed out of bounds and the Enlightenment slogan was, "Dare to know!" Enlightenment liberalism in this strain can be applied to many fields. The Scottish economist Adam Smith (1723–1790) believed in *laissez-faire* economics: capitalism should be left alone to run free without government interference. The British political theorist John Locke (1632–1704) and the American founding fathers who relied on his theories believed that free citizens should be equal to each other and not subjects of a crown that restricted their natural rights. The self-sovereignty of constitutionalism replaced a monarchy as the favored form of government. This desire for self-determination created the American Revolution, the French Revolution, the many constitutional challenges to other European rulers in 1848, the Russian Revolution (at least theoretically in its roots) at the start of the twentieth century, and the fall of Communism in Eastern Europe at its end.

What does Enlightenment liberalism have to do with the big picture of Catholic Church history in the modern era? As the Christian religion and the Catholic Church became less and less the glue of European society that it had been during the Middle Ages, many statesmen and believers no longer held that the Church should be closely allied with any specific state or government. And they had the quarrels and wars of the prior centuries to prove how dangerous religion could be in the wrong hands and when used for the wrong ends. So, while some Catholics held that the Church should continue to be closely aligned with a state and its policies—a position known as *integralism*—others welcomed the Enlightenment as an appropriate and welcome (if late) separation of religion from politics. It can't be denied, in the end, that while some leading voices of the Scientific Revolution and the Enlightenment in the seventeenth and eighteenth centuries remained Christians or at least Deists (believing in a generic and distant God), many of the European and Latin American political up-heavals that followed in the nineteenth and twentieth centuries were quite—sometimes rabidly—anticlerical.

Another major aspect of the modern church's big picture is the third wave of evangelization in church history after the first spread of Christianity via Paul and the apostles in the first few decades and centuries after Jesus, and then the second expansion throughout Europe during the Middle Ages. This third wave of Christian expansion overlaps the Reformation centuries since Columbus and Martin Luther arrived on the scene within a quarter century of each other. A kind of religious "cold war" spread around the globe: while Christians connected to various churches physically fought in Europe, Catholic and then Protestant missionaries raced to establish missions in Africa, Asia, North America, and Latin America in a type of proxy war. (The Vatican groups central America and South America under the rubric *Latin America*.)

As early as 1493, Pope Alexander VI interceded to draw imaginary lines in the Western Hemisphere marking Spanish exploration claims off from the Portuguese, though in this case the competing monarchs were both Catholic. Almost immediately, questions arose about the indigenous people the explorers encountered: were they— called "savages" often enough—human or not? Could they be enslaved? Could they be catechized and baptized? We must remember with sadness, too, that some indigenous people were baptized under threat of slavery or death. By 1537, Pope Paul III declared that "Indians" in Mexico were, indeed, human beings who could learn, accept, and practice Catholicism, and who should not be taken as slaves even if they did not become Catholic. A sign of the period's confusion in response to rapid developments is the fact that Paul III was reversing decisions by one pair of fifteenth-century popes (Nicholas V and Alexander VI) who had allowed non-Christians to be enslaved and backing another pair (Eugene IV and Pius II), who had opposed slavery.

Missionaries became the Church's new heroes, not unlike the martyrs and ascetics of the early church—and sometimes just like the martyrs because some missionaries were killed for the faith. This was the case, for example, with the Jesuit North American martyrs who worked throughout what is today New York State and the area surrounding Montreal and Quebec in Canada. A lasting but easily overlooked reminder of these missions exists in the very names of places spread around the American Atlantic and Pacific coasts, and eventually inland, many of which give evidence of Spanish Catholic efforts to spread the gospel. We think immediately, for example, of St. Augustine in Florida, Santa Fe in New Mexico, St. Louis in Missouri, and a slew of places in California: Los Angeles, San Francisco, San Diego, and San Jose.

A big issue for these missionaries was inculturation: describing the faith to the people they met without watering down its essentials. Catholicism could be adapted, but theological doctrine could not change. Some cultures did not have a conception of a God who could die and come back to life, for instance, and Greco-Roman conceptions of sacraments and theology did not translate easily. The most successful missionaries tried to explain Catholic ideas in the languages of the people they encountered, as the Jesuits did in Brazil and Canada, where they instructed mainly the poor. In Asia, meanwhile, Jesuits struggled to import Latin categories into Chinese and Japanese by engaging the intellectuals and elites, drawing the attention of Rome in what became known as the Chinese Rites Controversy.

In 1622, Pope Gregory XV established the Sacred Congregation for the Propagation of the Faith *(Propaganda Fidei)*, which unified a number of Roman departments and efforts relating to missions dating back to the 1568 congregation of cardinals dedicated to converting "infidels," to use the language of that day. An important goal of the congregation was to help an indigenous church and clergy develop as quickly as possible to replace outside missionaries.

Finally, it is impossible to talk about the big picture of

modern church history without mentioning, just briefly for the time being, Vatican II (1962–1965), the largest and most influential church council in history. We will discuss Vatican II further in this chapter's last section on modernity's uniqueness, but for now we should note that Vatican II marked a series of paradigm shifts. Similar to the way the Scientific Revolution and Enlightenment changed the way everyone looked at everything, Vatican II changed the way Catholics, non-Catholics, and even non-Christians considered the Catholic Church and the world. Vatican II asked how the Church could be "the Church" within the lightning-quick changes of the modern world. It was as if the Catholic Church at Vatican II caught up to the better angels of the modern world's Enlightenment three hundred years later. The Church was trying to remain set apart as a beacon of faith in a time of doubt by embracing and yet spurning aspects of modernity. But let us look at the modern Church from above and below before returning in detail to Vatican II.

THE CHURCH'S HIERARCHY

Modernity has not been kind to monarchy. In the space of a few centuries, constitutional, republican, and democratic forms of government almost entirely replaced sovereign rule by one person. As far as the papacy was concerned, there were two levels of challenge to its authority. First, in the greater context of Enlightenment secularism, there were some outside the Church who saw the pope as just another monarch. Since other monarchs were having their divine-right basis of authority challenged, so too was the pope. Second, this practice of political self-sovereignty was shared by some inside the Church who sought a more participatory form of church structure and governance.

Nationalism, another aspect of the Enlightenment but with roots in the Middle Ages, competed with religion for a person's ultimate loyalty. Think back to Henry VIII of England. In the sixteenth century, his goal was not so much to split with Roman Catholic belief and sacraments as to make England its own Catholic country with himself as its head, combining religious and political power within his version of an integralist reign. It wasn't as if he was begrudging the pope's authority entirely; he simply saw the pope as a rival monarch. Henry VIII was asserting that the papal reach of authority did not trump the English crown's own power in its own territory.

Nationalism pushed religion aside as the glue of European society, and other monarchs (and some bishops) took Henry VIII's lead. In central Europe during the late 1700s, Emperor Joseph II appointed bishops, claimed the right to review (and therefore effectively to block or veto) any papal correspondence before it was delivered, and seized control of religious orders within his lands. In France, bishops and clergy seemed to side more with their government than with the papacy, issuing in 1682 the Gallican Articles, again with deep medieval roots, which kept the Catholic faith but blocked papal jurisdiction in France. A century later, the French revolutionaries tried to make clerics paid state employees. This tendency to form what were essentially state churches continued in Germany in the late eighteenth century with Febronianism, a clerical movement that said the pope should let bishops on site make decisions on the regional and national level. It argued that the pope should never act as a monarch but as a unifying presence in partnership with his brother bishops, deferring to their national synods and backing off when his actions or representatives were seen as interfering in local matters.

As constitutional forms of government came to be preferred and tried out within countries previously led by a king or queen, there was a movement to apply a more participatory system within other layers of Church hierarchy as well. In the United States, the so-called Americanism movement was an attempt to marry Catholicism with the kind of autonomous individualism that characterized the new country's soul. Part of this effort manifested itself in the trustees system, whereby parishioners claimed that they owned a parish and could therefore hire and fire their pastors, make financial decisions, and otherwise run the show. On a larger scale, when the American clergy, now citizens and no longer George III's subjects after the American Revolution, needed a bishop, they chose John Carroll in 1789, after asking *Propaganda Fidei* for permission to do so. Rome responded that this procedure was permitted "at least this once," but it ended up being a one-shot deal.

Faced with opposition from Catholic royal monarchs and some of its own bishops, it is not surprising to find the papacy fighting back, even after being seriously weakened when Popes Pius VI (1775–1799) and Pius VII (1800–1823) each spent part of their pontificates as Napoleon's prisoners. After dominating Western society for about a century, the Enlightenment was faced with a political and cultural restorationist swing that reestablished central authority at the Congress of Vienna in 1815 and contributed to Romanticism to counter rampant rationalism. So, too, did the papacy respond by reasserting its unique authority—monarchical, yes, but the papacy is not "just another monarchy."

Nationalism may have pulled allegiance away from the papacy, but an unintended result occurred: freed from national identity and entanglements, the popes could claim a higher allegiance that transcended borders. Ultramontanism described an affection and loyalty that traveled "over/beyond the mountains" (the Italian Alps) and flowed from the pope in Rome to his people and back again. In Europe especially, a fondness for papal authority returned, especially among certain members of the educated elite favoring restoration on all fronts. There were several reasons. One was a shocked reaction to the awful treatment of the Piuses by Napoleon. Another was a distaste for the secularism that was tainting society, including bishops and priests. A third was what always happens: a countertrend against a prevailing trend. A fourth was a particular form of nostalgia for a medieval integration of Church and state, albeit nostalgia often based on legend and a superficial understanding of what medieval society was really all about. A fifth reason was a growing focus on the pope as a man himself: for much of history, few knew the pope's name and even fewer had seen his face. Now, inexpensive reproductions allowed his face into every living room. A kind of idolizing developed around the pope and the papacy, which Rome certainly did not discourage.

Another development also had an unintended consequence. For centuries the popes had been shackled by their temporal role as head of the Papal States, a parcel of land through the boot of Italy running northeast from Rome. While this area did provide physical protection at times, far more often the administration of the Papal States had compromised papal leadership and decision-making because popes could not afford to anger enemies who might attack the people under papal jurisdiction. When the Italian unification movement called the Risorgimento swept through Italy in the middle of the nineteenth century, Pope Pius IX (1846–1878) retreated to a small area in Rome in and around St. Peter's Basilica—giving us the phrase "prisoner of the Vatican." In 1929, Pope Pius XI (1922–1939) and the Italian Fascist dictator Benito Mussolini agreed to set up Vatican City as an independent city-state. Losing the Papal States took away the worldly and political twists and turns that had bogged the papacy down, which allowed the pope's status as universal shepherd and moral judge to flourish, as it did especially during the pontificate of John Paul II (1978–2005).

Pope Pius IX was also in the middle of another response to a challenge to papal monarchy, but this one came from within his own ranks. To make the case that he was the supreme bishop who was not beholden to the decisions of his brother bishops, to Catholics individually or collectively, or to any other body, Pius IX called Vatican I (1869–1870). The major item on the agenda of this general council was the discussion of what is incorrectly called *papal infallibility*. In fact, the statement that Vatican I eventually promulgated refers not to the infallibility of the pope as an individual believer, but to the infallibility of his teaching authority when defining a matter of faith or morals in a formal statement called *ex cathedra*, meaning from his chair, which is an ancient symbol of this teaching authority. Battered at the beginning of modernity, the papacy had turned itself around to become a major player on the world stage once more.

THE CHURCH IN THE PEWS

Perhaps more than any other period except the church's first few centuries, modernity has been the age of the laity. As often happens in church history, when the church at the top is battered, the people in the pews do not fail to flourish, which is precisely what had happened in the late Middle Ages when there were three popes. What emerged during these years of modern change and revolution was a laity that was more engaged in a daily living out of the faith, especially when it came to issues of social justice. The laity is as active, engaged, and especially educated today as it has ever been.

Let's begin with spirituality, which developed in reaction to the Industrial Revolution, which began in England in the eighteenth century and spread to the rest of Europe, and then the United States in the nineteenth century. Populations moved from the countryside to the cities looking for work because factories centered several rural "cottage industries" under one urban roof to keep costs down and profits up. As a result, cities became crowded and workers were largely exploited. Think of Charles Dickens' work— *Oliver Twist,* for example—or Mary Poppins' street urchins: they represented the cast-offs of the Industrial Revolution, the women and children who were not considered to be human beings, but rather as "hands" or cogs in the production machine of industrial capitalists. There were no child-labor laws, wage controls, worker's compensation, safety regulations, or overtime. Who would look after the needs of the least among these workers? The answer was the Church, just as when Francis of Assisi had turned the Church's attention to medieval ghettos when a similar wave of employment opportunities moved many people in a short period of time from the rural hills to the expanding cities during the twelfth century.

In fact, this modern movement to tend to the urban poor and to put the gospel to work replicated the evangelical awakening of the Middle Ages. In the past one hundred fifty years, it has come to be known as social Catholicism or Catholic social teaching. Although the concern was bubbling up from below, the movement exploded when Pope Leo XIII (1878–1903), although an aristocrat with a monarchical edge, turned the Church's power to back the poor workers. His 1891 encyclical On Capital and Labor *(Rerum Novarum)* strongly urged factory and business owners to care for their employees' health, well-being, housing, wages, and safety. A good day's work deserved a fair wage. An honest worker should be treated with justice and fairness. Leo XIII's support helped trade unions and political communities to develop as interest groups, not exclusively among Catholics, and in turn service-oriented workers organized themselves around the globe. The most well-known were Catholic Action in Europe, led by the priest-workers, and Dorothy Day's Catholic Worker movement in the United States. Although Day began in an urban setting, New York City in 1933, her ideas and work quickly spread throughout the country because of the Great Depression.

It is no surprise to find that Saint Joseph, patron of the worker (specifically the manual laborer), enjoyed enormous popularity in these centuries. Several popes encouraged Joseph as a model, culminating with Pius XII, who made May 1 the feast of Saint Joseph the Worker (although Italians still make a special cream puff named *sfinge di San Giuseppe* in his honor on March 19).

Just as in the Middle Ages, lay activities were one and the same with spirituality: we have here again an activist faith in which people knelt in the pews on Sunday, but then rolled up their sleeves and got to work the rest of the week. Retreats and missions focused on Catholic efforts: these events were times to regroup, to hear the preaching and exhortations of retreat masters, and to be silent; but they also led to later activities and renewed apostolic energy. Because some trade unions had huge Catholic enrollments, there was a natural link between work and this kind of involved faith. As in the Middle Ages, confraternities of like-minded folks came together for festivals and rituals such as Forty Hours' devotions, Corpus Christi processions, and other traditional devotions that eventually fell out of favor after Vatican II in the late twentieth century, yet are now making a comeback in some areas—and never really lost their attraction in Africa, Asia, and Latin America.

Immigrants imported their national saints, devotions, and feasts with them, deeply enriching Catholicism in their new countries, such as the United States, Canada, and Australia. Feasts favoring particular saints, at least in the United States, were keyed to immigrant populations and their ethnic saints: Polish and German festivals in Chicago and Milwaukee, Saint Patrick's Day in New York and Boston, and more recently Our Lady of Guadalupe celebrations in many American cities. To serve these populations, bishops sometimes permitted national parishes within their dioceses: parishes centered around a shared language, culture, or ethnicity rather than geographic borders. Catholics of that particular identity attended these parishes rather than their "home parish." While these nineteenth- and twentieth-century parishes served an important purpose, their existence—often within a few city blocks of neighborhood parishes—is a major reason why many urban churches are now closing. The Catholics they served have moved to the suburbs, leaving a dwindling and often quite small congregation that cannot support a parish with a grade school and the associated costs.

New immigrants, often of Latino, Caribbean, or Eastern European heritage, have replaced these prior Western European immigrants, although not always in the same numbers. Nevertheless, these immigrants remind us that the Church must remain true to the poor, the blue-collar workers, those rising up in socioeconomic circles, and the newly prosperous who can provide different gifts to an older Church in order to enliven the faith. The challenges and faith are the same; only the languages have changed.

Certain devotions transcend time and place. Modern spirituality recovered a tremendous devotion to Mary, specifically to the Immaculate Heart of Mary that was logically linked with Jesus' Sacred Heart. The modern centuries have witnessed many Marian apparitions, and then the shrines built in those locations that became sites for pilgrims: France's Là Salette in 1846 and Lourdes in 1858, Ireland's Knock in 1879, and Portugal's Fatima in 1917. Popes took particular interest in Mary. Pius IX in 1854 defined Mary's Immaculate Conception. Leo XIII issued nearly a dozen documents on praying the rosary. In 1950, Pius XII defined Mary's Assumption into heaven. John Paul II effectively devoted his entire papal crest to Mary, with her traditional color of blue and a large "M" dominating the field. His personal motto was *totus tuus*—a complete devotion to Mary. John Paul II said he survived the 1981 assassination attempt when Mary diverted a bullet from his major organs. As a result of this influential pope's personal devotion to Mary, and perhaps as a swing back to traditional devotions to Mary—such as the rosary and May crownings—that had lost popularity in the last few decades, Marian popularity is clearly on a global upswing at the dawn of the third millennium.

Finally, modern laypeople are increasingly less likely to be passive members of the faith when it comes to the hierarchy. The old line that the layperson's job was to "pray, pay, and obey" was probably never more than an incorrect cliché, but certainly during the modern era laymen and laywomen have done far more than this. The latest *Code of Canon Law,* issued in 1983, notes that laypeople have a *right*—a strong word, indeed—to be educated in the faith. This education does not have to remain at the level of the most fundamental catechesis, either, but notes that lay folks can have the highest degrees in the "sacred sciences" such as church history, canon law, theology, and Scripture. The *Code of Canon Law* also recognizes that laypeople can voice their opinions on topics related to their well-being as Catholics to their leaders. Their effort to be heard has certainly been growing since the priest-pedophile and episcopal cover-up crimes became known in 2002 in the United States, although the cases have rocked other countries, too. At the moment, it appears that the laity has grown up and is tired of being treated like children, especially since laymen and laywomen long ago outgrew the Catholic ghetto. They are now looking for the kind of respect within their own church that they have earned and enjoy in the secular professions.

The challenge, of course, is to find leaders willing to listen, since greater lay education will naturally lead to a desire for greater participation in decision-making. In the nineteenth century, an English bishop scoffed, "Who are the laity?" Ironically, he was answered sharply by his fellow Englishman, John Cardinal Henry Newman (1801–1890), who replied that the church would look foolish without laypeople. Indeed, Newman was an early and strong proponent of educating the laity at the highest levels possible. About a century later, Vatican II caught up with Newman's ideas by mentioning the laity in a number of its documents, not just the one specifically devoted to laymen and laywomen. Vatican II's documents note that the family is the first teacher of the faith. Laypeople's mission and vocation are central to the Church's goal of spreading the faith and the message of salvation, a goal that all Catholics share by virtue of their baptism and confirmation. Pastors were encouraged to allow greater participation in their parishes—a development seen every Sunday with lay eucharistic ministers and lectors. Vatican II specifically noted that laypeople are well qualified to bring Christianity to their daily lives at home and at work, making them intimate partners with the Church's mission. These goals have sometimes been a struggle, as clericalism continues to influence some Church leaders. Women especially have not always been given their due despite the fact that as mothers, teachers, and catechists they build the Church from the ground up. Nevertheless, it may not be too much of a stretch to say that the twenty-first century just might be the century of the laity.

WHAT MAKES THIS PERIOD UNIQUE?

Before modernity, atheism was not an option. Yes, Socrates was accused of being an atheist in his trial at Athens in 399 BC, and we can find ancient Greco-Roman philosophers occasionally opting out of the dominant pagan belief system, but otherwise it was nearly impossible to live in a pre-Enlightenment world and not believe in something supernatural. This big perspective change—that one could believe that religious belief was unbelievable—took several centuries to occur and there is no direct cause-and-effect link. But once the Scientific Revolution steadily began replacing bedrock principles of faith with science and math, religion began sliding down the proverbial slippery slope. The human-God connection then experienced an earthquake-like shift, particularly with the Enlightenment.

For as long as anyone could remember—in fact, dating back even beyond prehistory—people of many cultures believed that divinity of some sort lived as superiors above humanity, but now humanity and divinity began to be seen on an equal level. During the modern period, and particularly in Christian Europe, God was pushed aside to a certain degree by philosophers and scientists, though not all were unbelievers. Sir Isaac Newton (1642–1727), for instance, essentially had a nervous breakdown as he tried to reconcile faith and science. Blaise Pascal (1623–1662) likewise never abandoned his passionate faith in a living God active in human events. But God was often pushed aside and the human person was placed in a central position, as exemplified by the statement by Rene Descartes (1596–1650), "I think, therefore I am"— although we should immediately add Descartes believed that he was able to think because he had been created by God. The ball was rolling, however, and landed with a big "thud" when Voltaire (1694–1778) declared that if God did not exist, he would have to be invented. Even worse, this was followed by the nineteenth and twentieth centuries' "God is dead" movement, led by Nietzsche (1844–1900) and other existentialist philosophers.

The result of this shift was—and is—that it can be hard to be a believer of any faith in modern times. It can be particularly difficult for Catholics who even now are called upon to defend themselves as real intellectuals who nevertheless believe in a transcendent God and follow a pope. Around the world, a certain anti-intellectual or faux intellectual fundamentalism competes not just with atheism but with a learned faith system; this fundamentalism challenges the secular status quo and at times that faith system's own leadership. This situation is not confined to Catholicism, as all Christian groups—plus Jews and Muslims—are likewise contending with challenging and even dangerous fundamentalism movements within their own ranks.

This new situation had implications beyond philosophical differences. Modern governments have largely separated church and state in a practical sense to the point that theocracies stand out as the exception and are often described as backward. This process by which a government would not favor a particular religion or religious institution is known as disestablishment. The goal is to be sure that, in a modern democratic sense, no one religion is favored or disfavored over any other religion in the marketplace of ideas and rights. The idea is therefore related to pluralism, which allows all religions an equal place at the table, and toleration, whereby all of these faiths must be accepted without discrimination. Pluralism and toleration are likewise children ideas of Enlightenment liberalism, although at moments in the past certain cultures did allow other faiths a measure of autonomy, at least in theory and for a time. Judaism was at times a permitted religion within the Roman Empire, for example, and medieval Muslims generally allowed Christians and Jews to live within their territories provided a tax was paid and no effort at proselytizing was made.

In addition, a modern policy practiced in constitutional societies holds that no religion can be imposed on anyone as a litmus test or a qualification for, say, public office or jury service. In a sense, the disestablishment clause cuts off ties between religion (any religion or no religion at all) and government. Once more, this made Catholicism and all religions operate in a very different context—one that was far removed from the state of affairs for millennia in which religion and the state were so closely intertwined as to be virtually impossible to untangle. Throughout the world, questions remain as to how a religious believer, Catholic or otherwise, could possibly leave his or her convictions at the door when entering government service. It sometimes appears as if a purely secular government is, in fact, hostile to religion in the public market, which is one reason why issues such as tuition vouchers (whereby civil taxes are applied to parochial school bills), gay marriage, stem-cell research, or abortion become so heated. Freedom *of* religion, it is often pointed out, should not mean freedom *from* religion. At this point, since we are still living in a time that has not yet turned into "history," it is not possible to render a verdict on the lasting influence of disestablishment, but clearly Catholicism is no longer the dominant milieu of society as it had been for about 1500 years after Jesus, marking yet another way that modernity is unique in the history of religion.

Many of these developments have made being Catholic difficult, but let's turn to positive elements of uniqueness for modern Catholicism. We should note, however, that much recent work in theology and church history is demonstrating more continuities than discontinuities in church history. Factionalism leads some to pit the Council of Trent against Vatican II, for example, but we are understanding more and more how Trent had certain innovative tendencies, at least in its committee discussions and for a few decades of implementation afterward. The "Tridentine church" as a caricature of a siege mentality and a church closed off and hiding from the world is unfair (as mentioned at the end of chapter 3), although after 1800 we do find a certain papal reticence to embrace aspects of modernity. Ideas such as Darwinism, constitutionalism, and scientific advances in archaeology and textual criticism sometimes challenged long-held Church positions on issues such as the Bible and its interpretation, models of behavior and worship that impacted Church laws and liturgies, and what we really know of the Church's past. Two popes lumped some of these positions and methodologies known as historical criticism into an alleged heresy under the rubric word *modernism*. Pius IX in 1864 and Pius X in 1907 each condemned a list or *Syllabus of Errors,* but a number of these methodologies ended up being vindicated at Vatican II since they had increased our knowledge of the Church's past, in Scripture and liturgy especially, and helped the Church rejuvenate herself at the end of the twentieth century. It is better, then, to look at Vatican II completing Trent, going further and perhaps picking up on its best tendencies and the places some of Trent's bishops would have liked to have taken the Church had they been living in another era, and had the Church not been hit hard by the Scientific Revolution and Enlightenment that followed Trent within a century.

Given this background and understanding, it is also true that Vatican II did introduce paradigm shifts that turned the Church's perspective around, though not necessarily on a dime. What happened was that Church leaders (popes, bishops, and curial officials) were embracing what had been bubbling in the Church's body for more than a century. There were several such shifts, some of which were genuinely unique and others of which were recoveries of earlier aspects of Catholicism. We will focus on three of these shifts: images of the Church herself, the Church and the world, and Catholicism and other faith traditions.

For centuries, the Church thought of herself in quite hierarchical terms, with the unfortunate result of a hierarchy of vocations with the pope at top and laypeople (especially women) at the bottom. But the Middle Ages had a far more complex and appealing image at work: the people of God were the Mystical Body of Christ, which was the Church herself. After the Protestant reformers questioned the notion of the Real Presence of Jesus in the Eucharist, the Mystical Body language shifted to discussions of the Eucharist and this rich image of the Church was lost. The

idea returned, however, when Pope Pius XII, in a 1943 encyclical On the Mystical Body of Christ *(Mystici Corporis
Christi),* described the Church as the Mystical Body of
Christ, although he did not fail to note that Christ—and
therefore Peter and Peter's successors, the popes—is at the
head and that the bishops were the Church's "nobler members." At Vatican II and afterward, there was a renewed
emphasis on the Church as the people of God in fellow-
ship with each other and all enjoying unique vocations
that shared in the Church's goals of spreading the faith
and being Jesus to other human beings, be they Catholic
or not.

A related element of recovery was the idea, reaching
back once more to the early and medieval centuries, of
the Church as a pilgrim on a journey to God. The notion of the Church as a pilgrim and of each individual
Christian life as a pilgrimage allowed for a more open
approach to reassessments of past actions, identification of mistakes, acknowledgment of errors, and course
corrections. The image of the Church as a pilgrim is a
humble one that surely allowed the climate to change,
which is one reason why Pope John Paul II was so vocal
in acknowledging the Church's past errors and in asking God for forgiveness. Given the foibles of Christians
over the centuries, it is much easier to understand how
people made the decisions they did given their circum-
stances when one realizes that no pilgrim ever has all the
answers or knows precisely how near or far he or she is
from the journey's end.

Second, the Church rejected those times in the

past when it turned away from the world—the old *contemptus mundi*, to look far back, and the papal syllabi of errors from the more recent past—and instead asserted in the Pastoral Constitution on the Church in the Modern World *(Gaudium et Spes)* that the Church and the world had nothing to fear from each other. Both the Church and the world could give and take good things in a shared dialogue that went beyond simple toleration or détente. While we have seen that the Church was often right in the middle of the prevailing culture, it is also true that the Church has always tried to be a corrective to trends that go against Church beliefs and morals. Pope John XXIII (1958–1963) wanted Catholics to read the signs of the times and the Church to keep up with them, but he never abandoned the ancient Church principle that religious faith is often a sign of contradiction to a materialistic culture that doesn't have its priorities straight. Certainly in the Enlightenment world that produced modernity, the Church often found herself at odds with culture and consequently, in an attempt to protect herself, closed off both the good and the bad from entering into Catholic conversation. Though this may have been the case at the Church's highest levels, it was not true in the universities and pews, sources from which *Gaudium et Spes* profitably drew.

Third, the Church drastically altered its relationship with other faiths. It is a regrettable fact that, due to implicit or explicit actions of the Church's leaders or members, the stain of anti-Semitism and physical violence against Jews and Muslims mars church history. Also, Catholics and Protestants spilled each other's blood, as we have seen.

Vatican II dedicated two documents to these subjects. First, the Decree on Ecumenism *(Unitatis Redintegratio)* noted that there was plenty of blame to go around, but reminded all Christians of their shared love of, and discipleship in, Jesus. The council urged Catholics and Protestants to work together, pray together, serve together, and learn about each other by focusing first on what unites them and not what divides them. Second, the Declaration on the Relation of the Church to Non-Christian Religions *(Nostra Aetate)* went beyond Christianity to discuss Catholicism's relationships with other faiths, the monotheistic Judaism and Islam as well as Eastern faith traditions such as Buddhism and Hinduism. The document acknowledged great respect especially for Jews and Muslims, who share with Christianity a common father in Abraham. *Nostra Aetate* shattered the past when it declared that not every Jew at the time of Jesus and no Jew since then could be indicted for Jesus' crucifixion. In recent years, this particular topic has seen both progress and reverses, with a huge debate about what Pius XII did or did not/could or could not have done during the Holocaust to save more Jews balanced by the tremendous advances made in Catholic-Jewish relations during John Paul II's papacy. And that, perhaps, is not surprising given church history's pattern of challenge and response.

Discussion Questions

1. Did anything about modern church history surprise you?

2. Did anything about the modern church strike you as particularly familiar in terms of earlier periods of church history?

3. What models and lessons might be drawn from the recent past as the Church faces the future?

4. Do you think the modern separation of church and state helps or hinders the Church?

5. How might the true globalization of the Church affect how she operates?

6. How would you compare today's papacy with that of the past?

7. How would you compare today's laity with that of the past?

8. Give a portrait of the modern church to someone who knows nothing about it. What three main elements would you emphasize? Why?

9. When modern Catholics think of the word church, what do they have in mind?

FURTHER READING

Alberigo, Giuseppe. *A Brief History of Vatican II*. Maryknoll, NY: Orbis Books, 2006.

Aubert, Roger. *The Church in a Secularised Society*. London: Darton, Longman, and Todd, 1978.

Bulman, Raymond F., and Frederick J. Parrella, eds. *From Trent to Vatican II: Historical and Theological Investigations*. Oxford: Oxford University Press, 2006.

Chadwick, Owen. *The Secularization of the European Mind in the Nineteenth Century*. Cambridge: Cambridge University Press, 1990.

Fisher, James T. *Catholics in America*. New York: Oxford University Press, 2000.

Neill, Stephen. *A History of Christian Missions*. 2d ed. Revised by Owen Chadwick. London: Penguin, 1986.

O'Connell, Marvin R. *Critics on Trial: An Introduction to the Catholic Modernist Crisis*. Washington, DC: Catholic University of America Press, 1994.

Sullivan, Maureen. *101 Questions and Answers on Vatican II*. Mahwah, NJ: Paulist Press, 2002.

Sullivan, Maureen. *The Road to Vatican II: Key Changes in Theology*. Mahwah, NJ: Paulist Press, 2007.

EPILOGUE

By way of concluding, let's note a few larger lessons that emerge from surveying two thousand years of developments according to our structure of the "big picture," the Church's hierarchy, the Church in the pews, and each period's unique elements.

First, viewing the big picture teaches us that the Church has never stopped trying to define and explain the faith in new ways. The early church had to decide what words to use to describe revealed religious truths and mysteries that cannot ever be explained adequately. When the medieval Latin church, thanks to her scholastic theologians, rediscovered Greek concepts through Aristotle, she was able to take ancient formulas and make them more precise. This academic effort occurred after the waves of evangelization when missionaries had to explain Christian ideas to polytheistic Greeks and Romans in the first centuries after Jesus, and then to pagans and Arian Christians in Western Europe once the Roman Catholic Church turned away from the east and south to look north because of Islam's spread. Catholics had to continue stating their beliefs more carefully in light of competing systems and questions during the Protestant reformations and then the Enlightenment.

Second, the Church's hierarchy has always been concerned with establishing, explaining, and maintaining its particular brand of divine authority. Sometimes, popes and bishops adapted existing models, as they did with the Roman administrative system, establishing an imperial-style church after the Roman Empire fell in the fourth and fifth centuries. So accepted was this system that the popes had to set up a papal monarchy to beat back challenges from secular monarchs claiming a measure of divine inspiration and legitimacy, too. When the modern world almost entirely turned against monarchy, let alone divine-right monarchy, to embrace constitutionalism, the papacy and bishops once more had to state and justify their basis of authority in a world that no longer recognized such systems.

Third—and this is the most striking aspect of church history—the Church in the pews has always stood fast even when administrative and hierarchical troubles have threatened the Church's stability. True, we have had periods when the faith of the people veered into superstition, but it is also true that a predisposition to faith and the supernatural never disappeared. The faith may have been simple, simplistic, even naïve and completely unlearned, but that does not mean it stopped being sincere. When atheism arrived in modernity, it appeared among the elites and educated people, not in the pews. Faith helped people survive during the outright hostile moments of Roman persecution, the long centuries of the Middle Ages and Reformation eras when Christianity was the glue of European society, and modernity's skepticism. The people of God may stumble, but they rarely falter entirely.

Fourth, while no period is absolutely unique, we have seen that the four eras were quite distinct. The early church had to struggle to establish its very identity, to articulate what it believed, and then to celebrate and live those beliefs. The medieval church's dominant cultural leadership will probably never be repeated. Let us hope that the Reformation church's fragmentation and religious wars are not repeated, either, and that Vatican II's steps forward in ecumenism and interreligious dialogue will continue to bind longstanding wounds and divisions. The modern period, including our own years, finds the Church facing the challenge of coexisting with an environment not always tolerant of religious faith at all, let alone Catholicism's specific beliefs and structures. Vatican II recovered the notion of a pilgrim church, which puts a humble face on the journey to God, and asked Catholics to embrace the world. In the past, the Church sometimes responded to hostility by turning away from that very same world. It will be up to future historians to identify and interpret which option the Church will choose now at the dawn of the third millennium.